THE CREATIVE, Covered

The Creative, Covered

ISBN: 978-1-7399323-1-2 (hardback)
ISBN: 978-1-7399323-0-5 (paperback)

www.dedegold.com
Instagram: dedegoldart
Twitter: @dedegold1

Design and Production: Catherine Williams, Chapter One Book Production

Printed and bound in the UK by CPI Group (UK) Ltd, Croydon CR0 4YY

For hearts in the arts, everywhere

x

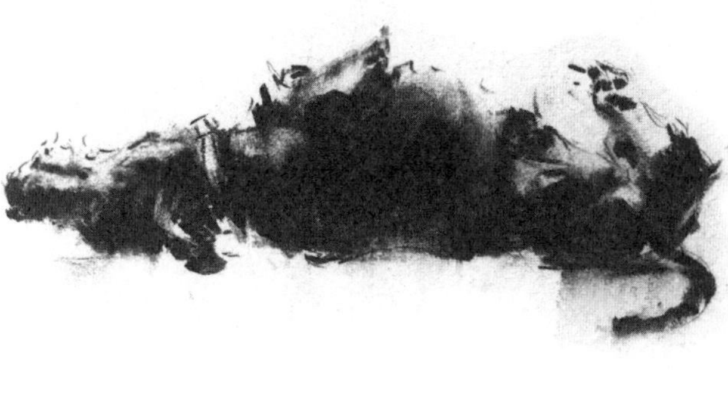

CONTENTS

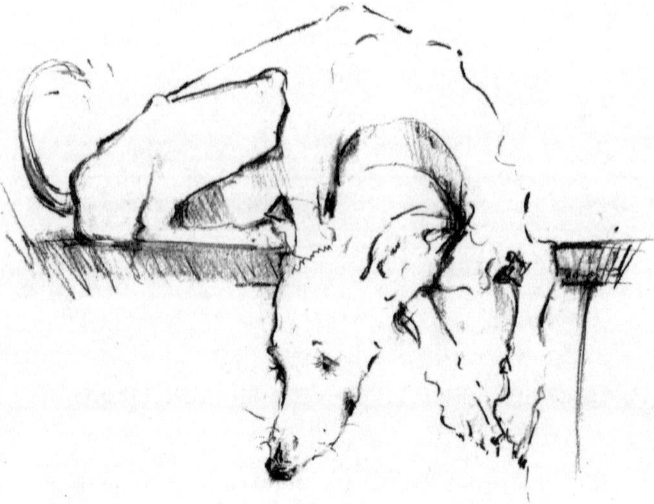

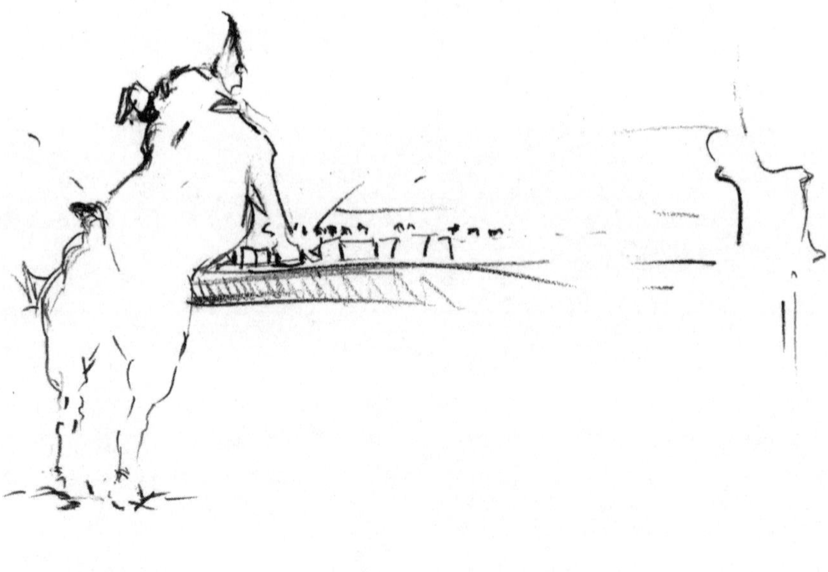

A PREFACE

I hate to disappoint, but the creatives I know are not capricious, hedonistic beings; in fact most artists I have met are extraordinarily sensible – we sort of have to be. I don't know a single diva, dramaholic or stereotypical hellraiser (sadly!) amongst us. Doing what we do requires serious application, utmost dedication, daytime waking hours, general sobriety and a reasonably balanced presence of mind. Often whilst balancing the needs of work and loved ones too.

We all hit hurdles when we choose this path; my hope is that this book will become a 'pick-me-up' for the days which test your mettle. In writing this I claim little originality, (ironically – see Chapter 3) but instead I'm collating the help that I have thankfully (and so gratefully) found or received along my own way, in the hope it will help you too. My first lesson on my first day in a law firm was that I didn't need to know all the answers – I just needed to know where to find them. Well, transferable skills! Here I am as a gatherer and a passer-on.

This book is intended as a retrospectively compiled roadmap which I hope will help you successfully blossom in your creativity, and live your creative life to the full. By 'successful', I mean to enjoy wholeheartedly its processes and the treasures that it yields, but also to step up and make your endeavours truly worthwhile. If you're going to give time – whether it's stolen moments or the full 24/7 – to your creative expression you owe it to yourself, and your work, to make it count.

It is written for those whose creativity is a glorious and welcome escape, and others like myself who have launched themselves headlong into the full creative hullaballoo. It is also for those teetering somewhere in-between. It is especially for those who encounter challenges in the experience of their creativity, to better understand why these are happening and how best to get through them, productively. If the learnings in my rear-view mirror can help replace your breakdowns with breakthroughs then I'll consider them well shared.

Although I write as one who has chosen painting as my artistic outlet, I believe the core creative process is universally adaptable for all who strive to express their creativity in *any* field. It is really all about what is happening 'within'; what is created 'without' is detail. So where I refer to 'art' and 'the arts' it is intended to refer to all creative outlets and outpourings. Dear musicians, writers, poets, perfumers, widget designers and milliners, this is your book too. The starting point and bedrock, the struggles and the salves are, no matter the media, all the same.

INTRODUCTION

To give a little context to this road trip, it's worthwhile beginning with a backdrop on where I'm coming from. In doing so I hope to give you a dash of courage to seize this life and celebrate your contributions and creative spirit in a way that took me so many years to do.

I had a lovely upbringing with my family in Ireland, studied law in college, and even moved to London afterwards to practise grown-up corporate law. It didn't transpire to be my life's calling but was, nonetheless, an interesting First Act. It presented me with my first lesson in self-knowing – or not. I was excruciatingly shy in university and I find it ironic that I now let it all hang out for a living. I would slink into the lecture halls (the other girls wafted …) and mostly leave again feeling super-anxious, irrelevant and rubbish on a daily basis. Everyone seemed so on top of their game, and to have life completely sussed, while I just wanted to disappear. Later I would head off to the Four Courts in Dublin throughout my solicitor apprenticeship and die a death as I stood in front of the judge. My mother, who was saving my life on a regular basis, told me to '*count to 10 and tell yourself your mother loves you*', so I did this religiously before launching into my High Court Thursday morning Motion Application.

You see, I was working always under the misapprehension that everyone knew so much more than me. With the wisdom which age and experience have given, I wish so much I could visit my 20-something-year-old self; I'd give her a good pep talk and tell her to speak up and flip some cartwheels. The truth is it's no good knowing the Constitution backwards if you don't have the confidence to carry it off. I realise, these many years later, that lack of confidence in your craft, when you've done the groundwork, is futile, redundant and a truly maddening waste. Just get on with being who you are, and stop worrying about who you are not. Anything else is a woeful squander, and those who matter are in your corner, always.

The romance bit. I shared a short marriage with a man I loved and am very grateful to have had that. We fitted a lifetime's laughs and intrepid adventures into four years – some may call that efficient. I wasn't an outstanding domestic success – I once remarkably buried the house phone whilst planting him a rosebush. He couldn't get through to tell me he was running late but appreciated the gesture, and the exquisite pink blooms. I believe now I was meant to head off down the path I've followed since and realistically, in my case, that would not have happened had we lasted the distance together.

I was devastated at the time by the breakup and it took me longer than is respectable to get over it. I had planned on being married forever and had zero Plan B. I had to look in the mirror (trauma enough!) and figure out who I really was. It was my beginning of 'waking up'; hell in the hallway, for sure, but it was ultimately what was meant to be for me.

A few curveballs and career U-turns later and finally I'm wearing my art top hat at last. It was either going to be gardening or painting – same mindset, different palettes. Now quite a few years since I first picked up a brush, my own life plans might have looked very different from those Mother Universe was plotting all along. But every tangent and cul-de-sac has led me to the here and now. It's not just the time spent honing our chosen creative skillset that counts, but the years becoming who we need to be when we get to our easels/desks/laboratories/pianos/tutus that matter even more. The growing pains are worth it once your paintings or your book or your music begin to get out there and stand on their own in the big world yonder – truly, there's nothing like it. Eyes to the horizon. Keep on trucking friends, even – no, *especially* – when it's testing.

And so to this book. The order of the chapters follow the natural course of the creative process. We start strong (best foot forward!) and with grit and wings we eventually finish in full heart. The journey in between can, however, require some exacting navigation. I identify the stages involved in the creative journey and the virtues and values, tips and triages that may help you at different turning points en route. I will call out the likely pitfalls you may encounter, and will do my best to steer you over and around them, with minimal abrasion to self and soul.

In **Section I** we look to tapping your inner creative – finding your voice and expressing your creativity in a way that is true to you. **Section II** thereafter looks at getting stuck in, whilst setting the scene for your optimum productivity. You will dive in full of gusto and determination that your artistic endeavour will be a mighty and rewarding adventure, with a healthy conviction that You Will Succeed. This is good and right and completely the attitude you need and I want you to have, every time.

Thereafter, just 'getting stuck'. **Section III** looks at the methods and medicines you might adopt when your creativity stalls, staggers, or all goes to hell in between. This getting stuck business happens for any one of a number of reasons, some peculiar to being a creative, some just to being human. It's better we understand them before standing square and shooting them down.

Getting out the other side of this 'stuckness' requires tenacity and courage and **Section IV** will help in putting the pieces back together in a constructive fashion. You have been through so much but here you are! You are doing ok. More than ok. This is all good.

Less dramatic than the BAD days are the incidental *not-so-good* days which go hand in hand with opting into creative life. Days when the fear creeps in and the courage seeps out. Fallouts from criticism, rejection, and lack of confidence will pepper the creative's path. Don't lose heart. **Section V** shares some thoughts on how to kick these chestnuts to one side leaving a clear course to your best creative self.

Chestnuts sorted, **Section VI** sees you braver and stronger, and diving full-on in. Whether your art is a source of pleasure or a source of income (and of course it can totally be both) we will look to putting this meaningful life, or meaningful *part* of your life, on a solid base from whence to soar. For those of you considering taking the professional plunge, I will take you through what you need to take on board before making your creativity your career. If continuing to create simply for creativity's sake, there are some pointers in here on sharing your work which will bolster your practice too.

Section VII will have you pitching for press and communicating about your creative shenanigans. **Section VIII**, finally, will have you pitching for your dreams. You've done the hard work, now it's time to believe in *it*, and in *you*. And for your audience to believe in you too.

I hope this book will be a life raft for you. Jump on board when you need it most to feel your creative pulse and tap your maximum artistic flow, or even just to find the joy in your creativity once more. For anybody who is creative or lives creative … with soul.

x

SECTION I: DISCOVER

There is a pulsing creative pilot light that glimmers deep within us all. Some will move through life to a different beat, not feeling the desire or necessity to call upon this part of themselves, but there it remains aflicker. An inner little engine fuelling our curiosity for life and our unique expressions of how we experience the world around us.

It can be an elusive little devil. Mine burns incredibly low at times, often (darn it) when I need it most. In practise it is less a steady little flame that we can fire up at will and more a scampering scarlet pimpernel that slips in and out of our reality unless we can harness it, hold on to it, and make it extra tempting for it to stay. There are always going to be times when a bit of investigative foraging and some clear focus might be called for to find your spark, or find your spark again. Once you do, you need to tend to it like your creative life depends on it – because it kind of does.

So let's get straight into the heart of this book. For the creatively curious amongst you – how to decipher your core callings and be true to your creative voice within? How to tap into your creativity, and thereafter, to keep it on tap? This is the creative's Holy Grail and nirvana all wrapped into one inspirational, and delicious, state of play.

Surely there's an app for that? Or at least a formula? Maddeningly, I have yet to find either. However this section will kickstart the investigative process to (re)discover those creative sparks, starting out on a path back to YOU.

Chapter 1 will speak to your inner scientist, **Chapter 2** to your inner Sherlock – both get elementary. In all endeavours you will want your self-expression to be, well, uniquely yours. **Chapter 3** addresses the balancing act of keeping you being creatively you.

Chapter 1

BEHIND THE SEENS

'You can't connect the dots looking forward, you can only connect them looking backwards. So you have to trust that the dots will somehow connect in your future because you have to trust in something; your gut, destiny, your life, karma, whatever ... because believing your dots will connect down the road will give you the confidence to follow your heart even when it leads you off the well worn path, and that will make all the difference.'

— Steve Jobs —

Entrepreneur, Inventor & Inspirer

I'm beginning to think we have much more of an idea of who we are when we are three than when we are thirty-three. Coming home one day from playschool I suggested to my folks that my name be changed. As far as I was concerned, enough time had passed for me to know my given name wasn't really me. I wasn't at all precocious, just serious, and I must have given a bit of thought to what felt to be most myself. I'm back to that way of thinking now with many more life skills (and disasters, triumphs, and flat-liners) under my belt.

It strikes me that as life happens, we build up our game faces and protective facades in many painted layers. We become a troupe of conformers where performers should instead be. It is easier, generally, to take the road *more* travelled. Whilst this may be our 'necessary', it is not always our ideal. I'd ask you, as you read this book, to give some headspace to your ideal. Step away from the restrictive corsets of expectation, not only of others but also those that you may have built along the way. Open up to the possibility of another version of yourself. When we live within the constraints of conformity, our sparkles get stifled and we default to automatics – not always wrong, but not always you.

To get back to the essence of what we're really about there might come a point when nothing less than a mega look in the mirror and an incisive line of self-enquiry will do. Back to that straight-shooting three-year-old beneath.

Creative Bones

I am taking it as a given that you are a Creative (heck, I'm giving us a capital 'C'). Not only have you picked up this book, but we all come into this world 'creative', although only a few of us will hang on to that kite string and let it pull us along its windward way. As you read this you might be anywhere on the creative spectrum: in denial, in contemplation, in confusion, in recovery or in your stride. Sometimes I'm the latter four in one day. Thankfully I've put the first to bed forever and I hope you will too.

The pickle is this. We all started out as *confident* little Creatives with an innate love of play. No one could burst our soap bubbles, and we loved an audience for our output when we nail-varnished the walls a smoking rouge noir. So what happened after that? The answer lies in life's obfuscations – a build-up of clouding layers to the point that we are unsure of what lies beneath, or what was ever there to begin. There comes a time (now!) to get out that bottle of acetone and gently wipe away the many coats until we reveal who we really are. And going forward – who we are meant to be.

Elemental

Go back to your drawing board. Find what is elemental. Artistically off-brand perhaps but the 13-year-old me was fascinated by the Periodic Table on the chemistry lab wall. Those mystical elements of undulating names whose compound permutations are the basis of *everything*.

If I draft an elemental blueprint for my creativity lab wall, my Hydrogen and Helium – pole positions 1 and 2 – are *Truth* and *Trust*. Being a functioning Creative requires a solid foundation of both. Your Truth is your first creative component. It is what is really you – the you beneath the expected, learned, and possibly 'safer' you. Trust is what is required of you to cajole it to the fore – trust in your authentic self, trust in your potential, trust that things work out for your highest good and trust that to not try is to not live the full life you were meant to.

Being 'in your element' is to know real happiness, to be at one with that which you truly are. It is to be in your own true deepest nature, so you need to go back to this. Your desire to create may be many things – nagging and persistent/nuzzling and nudging/head wrecking and de-stabilising/exciting and propelling – and multi combinations in between. One thing it will always be is your voice of truth within, whispering, calling or demanding to come out.

Delighting or de-railing, what you do with this is up to you. Consider giving it space, perhaps a microphone, even a beatbox – it might be the smartest, and possibly the most life-enhancing thing you ever do.

Chapter 2

FINDING YOUR VOICE

'Live your life in crescendo. 'Crescendo' is a musical term. It means to play music with ever greater energy and volume, with strength and striving. The opposite is 'diminuendo' which means to 'lower the volume', to back off, to play it safe, to become passive, to whimper away your life.

So live life in crescendo.'

— Stephen Covey —
7 Habits of Highly Effective People

When you speak, your voice is recognisable to those who know you – regardless of the words you use. Similarly, your creative voice is your individual artistic expression that is distinctly yours, identifiable as distinctly 'you'. It is, in essence, what sets you apart from others who do what you do so that others know it's you. Your 'style' is a broader brush. The way you express yourself may be shared by others of like minds, tastes and influences in your field. As you grow you will establish and settle into your style and use it to convey your voice – that which is uniquely you.

So – your voice. Do you know yet what yours sounds like, or have you still to even catch a note? Perhaps you're hovering about the starting line unable to begin? Or worse, thought you had found it, only to lose it as it crept back into its shell … Oh hell.

Let's start gently – pianissimo. Early endeavours will involve a 'push-pull' of effort and observation in working out what form your creativity naturally takes. Only then can you discover how to express it in a way that is true to you and that does your creativity proud.

This might come entirely organically to you (or, if you're more like me, really not). Daunted? Don't be – this is exciting, worthwhile and self-nurturing – but definitely not always linear. Nor is a tango but that didn't stop Al Pacino – it's just a matter of breaking it down into steps.

Step 1: Check *In*

Your creative voice is not 'OUT THERE'. It is firmly, and snuggly, *in here*. Finding it is less an active pursuit and more of a gentle reveal from within. And of course, once you find it, this voice may need training and distilling and hard graft to polish it up to be a sparkler. But your true voice in its raw state is waiting within you, full of potential, and it's up to you to set it free.

Marvellous, easy, let's go. Call off the search, this should be fairly and intuitively straightforward. Except when was anything that involves being a Creative quite that pushbutton?

Step 2: Check Your Flow

You might try starting in reverse. You will know you have located your creative voice when you find yourself in 'the flow state'. You'll have heard of this but you will know it first hand when you find yourself fully absorbed, beyond distraction, or the pull of the fridge. You are in your own rhythms and 'at one' with the task in hand. When your creativity feels generally aligned to your true self, and natural in its expression, then you're in the ballpark. And from there you're in 'the zone'. Hallelujah. So, working backwards, you want to align your creativity with what naturally feels good whilst following the flow of your creative intuition – it's a heart and soul thing.

If time travelling isn't in your box of tricks and you have trouble with this backwards methodology, it's time for a short self-inquisition. Don't rush these questions – let them percolate, play with them, sleep on them. Our true answers may not be on standby and gunning to the fore; our 'go-to' responses may need to fall away.

I suggest pulling out a journal, a pen, and a bun:

- What is it about my creative expression that brings me joy? (A cliché maybe but fundamental.)
- What keeps me curious?
- What do I do creatively that makes me feel relaxed and expansive?
- What do I do naturally and well and with passion? (Brain-storm this.)
- What keeps me in my creative headspace in a way that feels good to me? (Gin-storm this?!)
- If the pressure of earnings/others' expectations/life's laundry were thrown aside, where would my creative path lead me? (Dream-storm this …)
- What would I set out to create if I could take a free pass through my own self-doubt to the feel-good sunshine at the other side? (Go mad here I dare you.)

Step 3: Check Your Creative Courage

Ideally, once you detect the encouraging early whispers of your creative voice you can rejoice, make a game plan and crack on with confidence from there. Again, lovely in theory – tough in practice. The problem is that even our deepest best instincts tend to seek approval from our heads (rarely given), and this is where things get all jammed up. In order to get things flowing you need to build the bridge between *'I'm staying snug in my shell'* (no …) and *'It's going to be interesting to see how this pans out …'* (definitely yes!)

Cue your courage:

- **Remind yourself why you are doing this**: Could it be because not to would be to defy your very DNA? Perhaps because it makes you feel happy? Or because it might make someone else feel happy, or even simply feel? It might be because it's an antidote to life's laundry, and laundry sucks. It might even be because creative expressions can be a real force for good, and we need these; we need creative thinking and stimulation and innovation and the beauty of the arts more than ever. And if none of these strike a chord, 'just because' is quite enough.
- **You don't need an end destination starting out**: We often feel a need to justify our creative 'indulgences' (in truth they are an intrinsic part of being human) by knowing where we are going with our practice. You might be one of the lucky ones with a specific direction in mind and know what it is you want to 'say' from the outset. If you do have a specific statement to get out to the world through your chosen art, that's fantastic. Use your medium as a vehicle to fast-track you there. But if you don't,

that's equally valid and probably more the usual state of affairs – it was certainly mine. You might find that just working with a medium you are drawn to is plenty, and see where it takes you down the line.

- **Hook yourself into the 'now'**: Much of our self-doubt comes from facing new territory, which brings natural apprehension. Occasionally we also have the double-whammy of blush-inducing flashbacks to where things might not have gone so well before. As far as you can, feed your energy to the adventure, not the anxiety, and forgive yourself the minor mismoves, and even the whoppers. We blush, we learn, we move on …
- **Silence the Inner Critic …** There will inevitably be times when you need to convince your inner critic that you really don't need his help right now – thank you but no, you're doing just fine. If you can remain centred in yourself, parking judgement while coaxing your creative voice along, there should be no need for a scene.
- **… and his friends when you need to**: Many Creatives have another inner roommate. Although this one is overly cautious. Once again, make a call on when to listen and when to ignore. Know that your self-doubt can be a good thing, if you use it to help you. It is healthy and self-protecting to question our output as we go and it can save an unnecessary heartache or humiliation later. Use it to serve the purpose of keeping your standards high – but don't tip into it as your default when in fact you're doing just fine. Making a friendly alliance with your self-doubt will keep you serving up your best.
- **Be sure to call on your cheerleading inner roommates**: You know – the ones that make you feel like you can do anything? We

sometimes forget to ask them along when we are feeling less than brave – these are your VIPs.

Step 4: Check Out You …

For a moment let's place the rather serious concept of 'finding your voice' to one side and look instead to *sussing your style*. It conjures less onus, urgency and demand for something ground-breaking to come out with. It also suggests the swish of a Hermes scarf over your shoulder which is never out of fashion. And it rhymes with smile. (As well as 'takes a while'. But let's focus on the smile.)

Sussing your style will require some homework:

- **Do a recce**: At the very beginning look beyond yourself to those in your field you admire. What is it about their work that sparks something in you? That speaks to you? That resonates with you? That moves something in you? I think you'll find there's a bit of a conversation going on in there that shouldn't be ignored. Break down that composition, that palette, that riff, that sequence – what connects with you will likely be that which mirrors something within you, getting ready to come out.
- **Practise**: Stop thinking and start to really throw yourself in. Again and again and again. Don't be precious, be prolific; get some miles on the clock and see what flows, with zero pressure on the results. You will find your style in the dynamite three-way combination of authenticity, non-judgement and practice. Work from the heart, not the head, in the safety of your own good company and see what emerges. Your creative cream will rise to the top. What's not really you, let fall away. Just keep turning up.

- **Experiment and explore**: Enjoy the Muses and media you are drawn to – adopt some, adapt some, ditch some, mix some. Hone your skills, again without any endgame pressure, and see how it feels. There will be time enough for the deep analysis.

- **Self judgement**: Park, park, park. You don't want to have a quality crisis on top of your identity crisis – this is just a process you are going through for now.

- **Valued judgement**: Take, take, take! We need information to grow. At one critical learning stage I would always wipe down my ailing efforts before they could be critiqued at the end of class so of course I couldn't benefit from the help of those who had that expertise to see where I was failing. How foolish was that? My insecurities and pride got in the way of my growth. Don't be younger me.

- **Be true**: Whatever form it naturally takes, follow it. If it's not authentic, it won't be easily sustainable, nor will it connect. If you express yourself in a way that feels right to you, in a style that feels natural to you, that's really promising. In order to thrive in your art you need to create and be and move in this world in a way that is natural to you, always. I love that designer Tom Ford, in his earlier days of studying architecture in Parsons NYC, found that he was always working a dress into the design somehow. He swiftly switched to fashion – the writing was ever on his (wardrobe) walls.

- **Relax**: If you are worrying about finding your creative style please don't – it will come. As discussed, we are innately creative as a species and as long as you remain authentically you, and give it time and nourishment and half a chance, you can't help but arrive at it naturally. Relax, but keep going!

- **Persevere**: Keep developing that voice/style/identity crisis! There's always further to go. There will be points along the way when you will need to push again beyond your comfort zones. You have to be prepared to fail in order to grow if you want to keep reaching new levels and dimensions in your work. Open yourself constantly to the powers of inspiration and just see where your practice, and the outside forces, take you. They took me to the dogs.

Step 5: Check Out Me! (Ok only if it helps you ...)

I found my creative voice when I allowed myself eventually to indulge the curiosity which was tugging persistently at my sleeve. It wanted to play when I was sensibly ensconced behind my law firm desk. If I am being honest something bigger was moving me on. I wanted so badly to be the professional I had trained to be, with all the stability and security that it would bring, but I was going against my own flow, and wellbeing, trying to make it fit. My skin went to pot, my head ached and I found it hard to ever sleep. In a way I hadn't much choice when I finally put my suits away. I had to work out another way to roll.

I hit roadblocks almost immediately, particularly with the small matter of my own expression. 'What do you want to say?', an art-world friend asked. Dear God, I felt rabbit-in-the-headlights stuck. I knew painting was something I wanted to do but I didn't feel authority enough on anything much to give grand gestures or to make any important or political statements. But what I have come to know since then is that what I was doing, what felt right, what felt 'me', was plenty reason enough to keep going. I started to explore my creativity – to engage with it, to at least listen in to it – because I knew I was missing something in my life. (Plus I had an apartment full of empty walls, so I reckoned I'd give it a whirl even though I didn't have a plan for world peace.)

One day then, not so long after I really started painting – I met someone. They always say it's when you're least expecting it and you'll know when it clicks. They're right. He was a liver-chestnut perfectly spotted dalmatian in Battersea Park. He knocked me sideways – in a very good way. Heavenly to look at, but so much more than that – his energy was pure four-legged polka-dotted magic and it was the first time I thought: '*I want to capture THAT.*' I wanted more than anything to catch the *feeling* he gave me. So, *this* was inspiration! I had read about such moments with envy: faked it, feigned it, even felt I knew it, but here it was, at last, and life switched up from there.

I sought to find the most effective and worthy way to hold on to it and channel it. I knew it was the beginning of something exciting – for us both. That dalmatian polkaed his way onto the walls of a beautiful Bond Street store, and that happy encounter was the starting point for me.

In my art thereafter I set about painting souls, and soulfulness; the feeling these glorious animals give me, conveying their essence, not their every whisker or hair. For me in every composition the starting point is not about a 'likeness' but about a feeling and doing my best to commit that feeling to canvas, in the hope that others may feel it too.

What is it *that speaks to me* and makes me want to paint? Or to finally answer my art-world friend's: 'What do you want to say?'. I'm trying to see into these gorgeous souls, and there (hopefully) comes a moment of curiosity when they try to see back into me. It can take some time but usually, eye to eye, four-legged to two-legged, there comes that point and they let me in.

In early days, a girlfriend frankly confided that she had pretended not to know me when she saw me lying on my tummy interviewing a divine but introverted dachshund at a smart Kings Road café. Well needs must and I will never not swallow my pride for an irresistible set of whiskers. These were the humble and at times humiliating beginnings in finding my voice.

In our various creative expressions we all aspire to finding our individual inspirations, style, tone, eye levels(!), nuances and ultimately voice. We want to know who we are creatively, and who, indeed, we are not – self-discovery at its magnified and most satisfying best.

For now, enough about me, and more, much more, about you.

Chapter 3

YOU DO YOU

'Be yourself. No one can say you're doing it wrong.'

— Peanuts —
Snoopy

To be a happy and lifelong Creative you need to find a way to be yourself in your art. We all set out in the name of 'originality', of course we do, but if in the starting blocks that sounds like a tall order, just commit to being authentic – that's the extent of the brief to begin. Let me explain:

Strictly speaking, being original means coming up with the earliest form of a concept – a unique, 100 per cent new, one-off, first-born version of your idea, in its purest sense. This isn't easy. And the problem then with *trying* to be original is that the pressure to come up with something entirely new can present you with a massive block before you've even begun.

Being 'authentic' is to be true to your spirit and to yourself. That's it. If you can manage this you won't go far wrong. When you create this way there is really no other judge that matters when communicating *your* self, *your* soul: the essence of *you*. When you work authentically, your truth is there on your paper. Or on your laptop or in your kiln or in your ballet steps. Whatever your art form, seize the opportunities it offers to express what's really you.

Starting Block Blocks

Many of us worry that it has all been done or written or produced before. Worse still, we can often find that as we create, other Creatives are hitting similar notes simultaneously. Maddeningly they can also seem to be doing it better. Cue a self-berating spiral.

Another downer is that these days of mass dissemination also mean that so much is coming at us all the time – to be read, listened to, seen and shared – that it's hard to avoid being influenced even when you try not to be. What are you going to do? You might consciously endeavour to be not influenced, even subconsciously; or you might – less consciously – stay in bed.

We know we must keep striving to create authentically, and we know we must keep getting out of bed. Here's how:

1. **Tap your intuition**: Be more intuitive and less cognitive in creative mode – more soul than brain. This might not come naturally to you, for me it's an on-going struggle. I'm a numbers girl – I like geometry and the tidiness in seeing proof that it all adds up. Leaps into the unproven and unknown unnerve me. But work with yourself on this.

2. **Tap your inner Titian!**: (Or any other gutsy Creative …) Titian was a ground-breaker. He went bold and bright and luminous and left his contemporaries needing shades. He broke the equivalent of the Renaissance internet. He DARED, because bigger and bolder and richer felt true to him, to express the world he saw around him. Sometimes you need to dare too. The Creative's

journey involves taking risks, being a little brazen and yes, at times feeling damned foolish having done so. Put your pride and ideals of perfection in the back seat and take your inner Titian for a trip.

3. **Find your primal**: By 'primal' I mean the most basic and important part of who you are. And of what you feel. 'Good' art is not an automatic rendering of what your eyes see or what your mind thinks – it's about how your soul responds. THAT is what is interesting and keeps it authentic *and* original and should be the starting source.

   To create is to do more than 'replicate' your subject matter – what is important is how you feel about it. What is *of interest* to **you**? Alla prima maestro Richard Schmid puts it beautifully: 'Do not ask yourself, "***What*** do I *see*?" rather ask, "What do ***I*** see?"' Drop the specifics to the degree that suits your vision. And to the degree that adding them would only clutter what you wish to express. Run with the spirit of it instead. I'm not saying go full-on Mondrian, but absolutely do if that's you. Your creative expression should not be bound by your source of inspiration, only ignited by it. For the non-visual artists' media, what do ***I*** hear/feel/perceive? It is *your* emotional response to your subject of inspiration that will make the good things happen. All creative works are responses to specific stimuli – use them as starting points and see where they take you. Be guided by them but never compelled. Call deep within yourself throughout your process and listen in. Birdsong, that sweetest of sounds, is primal. Find your birdsong.

4. **Use your inner landscape**: This is the backdrop against which your creativity sparks. Your creativity expresses itself in context of that which you already are. Authenticity draws on our inner

fabric and we are essentially an intertwined mesh of all we have been so far. These influences (past and present) naturally bleed into our own styles and go towards making our art uniquely of us and ours. Rapper-singer-songwriter Stormzy shows us how, in all his activist and philanthropist glory. He not only draws on, but delivers on, his experiences of his world in his work. And brilliantly he is using his voice to change the landscape for those coming behind him.

5. **Use magic beyond mechanics**: Your techniques in your creative practice should be strong – these are your foundational tools. Don't, however, remain slavishly tied to them. Learn them, hone them, and then adapt them to your ideas as they come. Develop new techniques. Remember the real beauty happens when the spirit and the craft come together.

6. **Shake it up**: You will want to bring your own independent and creative approach to your work. To do this successfully you may need to turn all the information in your head, on its head. We get bogged down in the boring tracks of routine and inherited patterns of thinking. Begin to ask bigger questions of your creative self. We have a library full of mood boards and memories within us (and our shoeboxes if you've kept them over the years like me) to draw from if we have been around a while. Rummage and mull and see what they spark within you.

7. **Make it up**: Why do we leave our imaginations hanging in the cloakroom of grown-up life? When was the last time you really took a head trip? There are days when you need to go lie in the grass and let the ideas freewheel … To imagine is to leave behind the shackles of the mental processes of conscious thinking. It is to use

parallel processes of the unconscious mind – the image-making processes – to envision something new. There are idea triggers all around us – you just have to train yourself to capture them. Make up your mind to pay attention. Notice them – connect them – toss them around a bit and see how they fall back together. See what sparks again. Look behind and beyond the things you see and the people you meet – inspiration is everywhere.

As a teenager I was living life at eye level until my fifth form art teacher, Mr Garbett, told me to 'look up'. Hardly revolutionary, but it kind of was to me. He urged us to keep looking up when we walked through our hometown – the old buildings above the shopfronts, the dishevelled elegance above the '80s mishmash streets of commercial necessity and the stories they might have told. Look up.

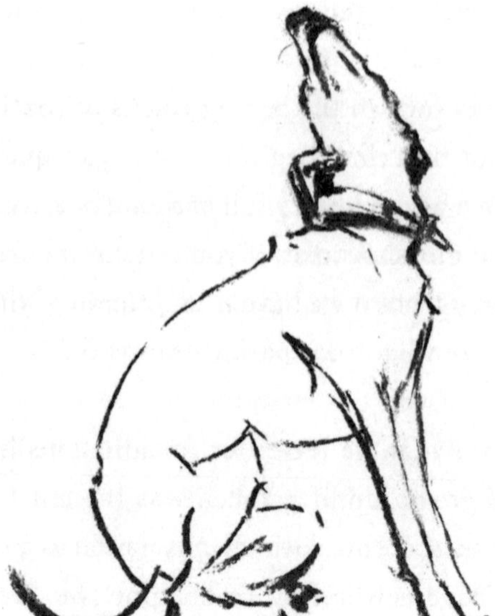

8. **Map it up**: When I'm drawing a blank, I go back to the drawing board, literally. As in school, pigtailed, aged eight, my essay title in the middle with word bubbles coming out and letting my mind express everything that's coming up. Write down some ideas (then more ideas to get better ideas …), pick the best, discard the rest, forgive yourself the ridiculous, and you've begun.

   Many Creatives use this mind mapping process – Bob Dylan loved the free word association of brainstorming – he would write just what came into his mind and the good stuff flowed easily, without overthinking (he warned against this!). But I guess he was Dylan. Still – gut, instinct, soul.

9. **Soak it up**: Glean what you can from all around. I already recommended doing a recce in developing your style and you may have heard alarm bells. It might have struck you as counterintuitive in striving for originality as to detour you from your authentic instincts. Please know that it is healthy in your creative development to be open to what has gone before, what is happening now, and what is all around. Observe who you are in these contexts – your tastes, your soft spots, your perspectives – and then be open to your response to it all.

   Enjoy the work and learn from the processes of your creative heroes and peers. Roll in it, soak in it, then shake it down. Appreciate, enjoy, learn and *build*. Be part of a movement! Put together all the mighty knowledge and experience and inspiration you are gathering en route. You will find that certain elements (tones/nuances/styles/combinations/palettes) resonate with you quietly again and again. Keep gathering your thoughts and responses, and you will see the patterns emerging. This germination stage is beautiful and important. Wear your ideas for a while, let them incubate and see how they feel. Your artistic expression will be the ultimate synthesis of all your instincts, experiences and influences as you creatively grow.

Writers must read, painters must go to galleries, singers to songfests, dancers to dances. Be willing also to jump outside your box – crossing creative disciplines is a potent inspirer. The ever-excelling milliner and creative king of his craft Philip Treacy says: '*I believe in originality, primarily. However, it's important to know what there has been before to aim in that direction. Art history informs us. It informs our mind. I like to look at books, exhibitions, paintings, as a computer, subconsciously taking on information*'. He embraces art history in the fuelling of his indisputable originality, all to spark the starting point inspiration of his next champion chapeau.

As you then go on to develop and create your own unique work, of course have your hand on the handbrake for when you feel you are tipping out of your own authenticity. Others' influence may be invaluable but you want to make your masterpieces and melodies your own. You will know. There will come a point fairly early on when the last thing you want is to take on or practise another's voice or style. When the time is right you will automatically stand away from others' influences and want to steam ahead in your own zone and in your own unique way. Reconnaissance done, stabilisers off, pedal ahead.

10. **Stoke it up!**: An exhilarating part of the Creative's brief is that you get to interpret the things that are before you and happening around you and put these into your work. If you plug in and follow your own true responses, it's a pretty safe bet that you will create something new.

Conclusion: To be the real deal Creative, create your own rhythms and nurture your own style. Be your own pioneer. Don't shy away from the unfamiliar, instead welcome it in. Zag when others zig – yes – but only when zagging is authentic to you. You don't need to be different *just* to be different. You need to be true.

Aim for awesome and always be yourself. There's a serene lady where I live who I see when she goes out to buy the papers. She must be late 80s if a day and is the epitome of English conservative old-fashioned respectability. Right down to her silver glitter Converse baseball shoes.

Always, ALWAYS, come back to being
your unique, one and only, you.

SECTION II: UNCOVER

The beauty of the investigative process is in bringing to light what has been hidden. Connecting into your creative self is exciting, but more exciting still is coaxing it forward to see the light of day. This section explores how to build a creative practice in a context that supports both it and you.

Physically, mentally, soulfully, you want to be your best trainer, life coach and guru. This may sound hardcore (and exhausting) but it will be worth the effort, I promise.

Chapter 4 should help to set the scene: you need to find your balance before getting your turbo boost on. In **Chapter 5** we'll look at certain mindsets which I hope you'll find helpful to keep turning work out (and to keep you actually turning up). A warning about **Chapter 6**: you might find it a little trippy … but please don't jump ship! You might surprise yourself (and your eagerly awaiting audience) if you are open to possibilities beyond the perceivably obvious.

Everything proposed is intended to keep you upbeat and productive as you unleash your creativity (ready world?!!) and to keep you keeping on.

Chapter 4

HOW TO BE PRODUCTIVELY CREATIVE

'I don't want to end up simply having visited this world.'

— Mary Oliver —
Poet

Let's make it count. Starting out, there are things you need to have lined up to give yourself every chance. If you want to be productive – and of course you do – and you want to tap into your best Creative – and again, of course you do – these are your starting tools:

Solitude
Gratitude
Self-Care.

Solitude

To be productively creative, you need some element of solitude. You might be paddling your own canoe by working alone, or have a single status lifestyle, and creatively speaking this can actually be a very satisfactory state of affairs. For those more entwined I am not, however, suggesting for a second that you up sticks and leave your partner/children/colleagues to fend for themselves. This would be drastic. You may need to just carve out some soul-enquiring time in an otherwise very peopled life. Wisely spent and focused energy can more than compensate when we are short on hours to spare.

Many of us fear solitude, which, although understandable, is misguided. Contrary to being a pitiful existence (as is so often the perception), it can also be a veritable blessing. If you didn't choose it and single status solitude is somehow forced upon you, then embrace it. More than that, commit to making the very most of it. Instead of fretting over the uncooked meals *à deux*, think of the New York City singletons where an oven is a welcome extra storage space for their dancing shoes. How perfect is that? Sculpt all night and have toast at 3 am with a cuppa and *Bonnie Tyler (*insert relevant decade power ballad) on repeat – BECAUSE YOU CAN.

The thing is, spending time on your own is really useful and important in developing a grounded sense of awareness. It is from this point that true connection with yourself is possible and thus it is the place from which good things happen. Besides, without valuable alone time, how can we mirror dance when the notion takes us without being judged (nay committed)? Or hotfoot it – without explanation – to execute 'the best idea yet' before it mysteriously leaves us in its wake a mere moment later? See? Solitude kind of rocks.

If you work or live with others it is vitally important to retreat to yourself sometimes, somewhere, somehow. Your creativity requires some element of isolation for it to thrive. Those of you in relationships can absolutely win the triple crown of creative career, partner in crime and kiddywinks, but my point is that your own company is good company in the arts, and is at times essential for the real soul stuff to arrive.

If you are flying solo, polish up your singledom savviness and embrace the life you are leading. It may be daunting, but it is also exciting, and it is *full of possibilities*. And if you've yet to decide that it's all of that, it's time to flip your thinking. You are a free agent – it's a fantastic launch pad – use this feeling of freedom in your work. Dare to cast perceived parameters and the weight of expectation aside – let it run and see where it takes you. *This is a really good thing.*

Besides, I think you'll find in the sense that matters, we're never really on our own. I have found the wider artistic community to be hugely supportive with a feeling of 'in-it-togetherness' wherever you connect with them all over the world. I regularly solve my materials, mediums or archival conundrums on artists' forums or by speaking with artists directly. One of the great upsides of Instagram is as a portal to see what's happening out there in Creativeland, and to join in. We have a common playground in this pan-global synergy of souls.

So if you're rarely alone, you will need to actively carve out some alone time to tap your creative wellspring, even if it's mere crumbs in your life cake. If you're sometimes alone, (a few hours in the day, everyone fed, nobody dead) go for it. When the moments come, make sure it's productive solitude. Sculptor and artist Dame Barbara Hepworth's work came to exemplify modernism, and her efficiency – apparently – the modern woman. She was caught off guard when she gave birth to triplets whilst only expecting one – no I can't imagine. But she stole herself away when she could, determined to do something focused on her art for the short spells she could find. The results: fewer sculptures but 'more triumphs'. Ask a busy person …

So while faffing about on Facebook is fun and all, there's a Higher Calling now, and you've got to answer it. And if you feel like you're always alone, I hate to break up your pity party, but (a) you're not – truly, no one is any more (sorry), and (b) you have no excuse not to show up, dig deep, get on with the dance and PRODUCE.

Gratitude

Gratitude is not only the keeper of a healthy headspace, it is the bedrock for a mentality of abundance and expansion. So, if you want to produce bountifully, be thankful, and then be thankful some more. If you have dived fully into a life creative, what a privilege and how very lucky you (*we!*) are. For those who enjoy creativity on a less than full-time basis, remember how wonderful it is to have this valuable added dimension in your psyche and your life.

Why is gratitude so important? Well for a couple of reasons (and not least because there is nothing worse than *ingratitude*). Humility is a virtue – a great virtue – and in being thankful for what we have, we are acknowledging both our modesty and our great wealth. But – and forgive me if I seem to go all dippy here – gratitude is also the best way to tap into the Universe. And believe me when I tell you that we all need to have it on our side.

'Please don't worry.
I've got you.'

— The Universe —

I realise that faith is the most personal of spheres but for me I find it important to start the day in thanking ... *something.* Call it God, or Source or the Universe or Fate, or just the good vibes (man) whatever you might perceive he/she/they/it to be. Whatever it is, it's something greater than myself. Two steps out of bed – *Thank* and *You*. Because there are times when – bear with me! – I know that my painting is coming from somewhere else. Somewhere a lot more interesting than me. When I'm on a roll and my brushstrokes are singing I instinctively feel that I'm not working alone, or sometimes not even vaguely in charge. Just as there are times when I need to know what to do next and it comes in a message

– somehow – someway. This happens when 'in the zone', with a feeling of direct connection with the work. When I'm not in the flow and generally not feeling it, or I'm tackling something important (a paw!) I take a few moments to check in and invite that something/someone else to come on board and help me take it from here. These days I regularly ask for intervention in my composition and brushstrokes when I'm feeling overly humanly and artistically flawed.

Gratitude is fundamental to how we live our lives. To my mind it is the bedfellow of all things warm and loving and kind, and it is ever self-perpetuating. The more grateful we are, the more that comes into our lives that we can be grateful for. It is an opening of the heart, soul and mindset to a vibration from which more to be grateful for comes. I totally get if this sounds too simplistic and will require for many a leap of faith – or at the very least a suspension of disbelief – but I truly believe it is fundamental.

Even in upside-down times, it is possible to be grateful for the smallest things. If you can, make it a habit in your day. Be grateful for the nudges and the moments that are waking us up. Be grateful for the upsets – instead see them as 'set ups', designed to promote our learning, growth and progress. And be especially grateful for inspiration when it comes tapping; open yourself to that magic and then allow yourself to let it come right in.

Self-Care

I know I sound like your mother here, but we Creatives are by nature sensitive beings and you need to take care of yourself. Resolve from the outset to look after your creative self – it will stand to you. Some days are easier than others, some days we need a little propping up. But less so if we have worked on making ourselves match fit to begin.

Find your balance and take this seriously – your creative motor needs a robust and reliable engine. Forearm yourself by keeping physically and mentally strong and energised, for your life's sake as well as your art's. For me, a good mix up of meditation/yoga/token exercise (outdoors)/sleep/fun (in increasing order of importance obvs.) is what works best. You'll know what works for you but here are some suggestions that may be worth a shot:

1. **Get out there**: Don't disappear. Solitude is great but isolation sucks. It's important to get out of your cosy nest and connect with people (and no, again, I'm not talking about Facebook here). Personally, I find that I get way too happy in my own company and often forget to bring the joy of an evening with friends or family into play. Laughter is vital. Some days, at least occasionally, swerve your best intentions and ditch the serious stuff: out with the Jung and in with the fun. Embrace the light-heartedness and sense of wellbeing we only get from sharing time and wine (or wine gums/an apple martini/an apple pie) with special people in our lives. It brings joy and a well-needed perspective into our, potentially, navel gazing bubble.

2. **Get practical**: Conjure up the best resources and creative space you can for those fabulous ideas to zing. When you up tools in the morning – be it pen, brush, laptop or feather boa – give yourself a sporting chance to achieve your tiptop performance that day.

   Organise your workspace. Creative challenges are upsetting enough so set up your set-up to maximise your chances at creative brilliance; a well-designed backdrop is crucial. I like a certain sense of order (not instantly apparent to the naked eye, granted) and to know where all is to hand before getting messy. You don't want to halt the creative flow to figure out where the typewriter or burnt umber is hiding. Few of us have our dream creative space starting out – or even know *what* our ideal space is – but no matter the dimensions or the décor, as long as it has a good heart you're good to go. Even if it has a broom-cupboard feel about it, there's no space so soulless that the right temperature, lighting, and sustenance won't transform into a productive hub. Install yourself into your creative nest and might I suggest a sign on the door …

'I'm sorry I can't meet your requests today.
It's just not your day.
Tomorrow doesn't look very good either.'

Aaaand…. Begin.

3. **Get resourceful**: Being realistic, if the best you can muster is hiding from your children under the stairwell to grab 20 minutes of pen on paper, or battling the Celtic rain at your plein air station, put up your metaphorical (and actual) umbrella there and then. Take it, go with it, heart up, head down AND MAKE IT THE BEST YOU CAN.

If you're really finding it hard to be upbeat and it's feeling like mountainous terrain, know that we have all been there. Challenges appear and then their first cousins come to the party. Try to switch it up. What can I learn, retrieve or salvage from this? There are always pay-offs for exploratory endeavours. The riches which will flow won't necessarily be those of the financial sort. But art and impecunity have long since gone arm in arm.

If this is the state in which you find yourself, don't let it be a barrier to keeping on keeping on. Firstly, you're not alone. Author Ben Okri found himself living in the park whilst studying comparative literature at Essex University. He didn't give up – he went and became the youngest ever winner of the Booker Prize for Fiction instead. And let's not forget a certain Miss Coco Chanel whose beginnings were anything but glamourous. Her father, a peddler, had to leave her in an orphanage when her mother died and the nuns there taught her how to sew. Later on a chilly winter's day in Deauville she fashioned a dress out of an old jersey – her first taste of design success – the rest is sartorial history …

Secondly, we are all by now practised in the art of belt-tightening, are we not? So, buckle up if necessary. Think outside the box about how you can give to your creativity the conditions it needs. Try to make it work – back to the recession reference material – baked potatoes go a long way in thin times and drink your water from the tap. (I gave up my morning café indulgences when the bank balance was less than balanced; on discovering this a very kind benefactor wrote me a caffeine cheque to keep me going for a year – he insisted that having decent coffee in my system was in the interest of great art!) My only caveat is that in doing what you do, try always to buy the best quality materials you can afford: a decent laptop or the best ballet shoes or worthy paints and brushes. There's no point pushing boulders uphill. As we'll be coming to soon, the artistic darkness can easily descend, so ward it off as best you can with conducive tools.

4. **Get some sleep**: Restorative, divine, sleep. You should also be aware of the added excitement it can bring in terms of inspiration downloads. The Beatles classic *Yesterday* came to Paul McCartney in a dream one random night in 1964: Albert Einstein found the theory of relatively in his. Keith Richards woke up one morning to find he had committed the Rolling Stones classic, 'I Can't Get No Satisfaction' to a tape recording bypassing a waking hour completely. Jasper Johns found his

flags, Mary Shelley her Frankenstein, Steinbeck swore by the problem-solving powers of 'the committee of sleep'. Are you seeing how this might work?

According to Berkeley University scientists, sleep stimulates our minds to make 'non-obvious connections' between memories, ideas and events that would not normally go together. The dreaming process associated with REM sleep, it seems, yields valuable fodder for our creativity for the daylight hours that follow.

Even my fascinating periodic table of chemical elements was delivered up in the realms of REM to the Russian chemist Dmitri Mendeleev on a February night in 1869. In his dream he saw the table in its entirety where the elements each fell into place. On waking he recorded it just as he had seen it, save for one place where a correction appeared to be necessary.

Keep that pencil by your bed.

5. **Get some beats**: This is a reference to the power of music as an accompaniment to creativity. I just don't paint without it. It's my non-negotiable and my wingman. My mood dictates the genre and the stage I'm at in a painting, the tempo. Every composition needs its quiet notes and when I'm finding those I will play something soft. Afternoon sessions require a rush of some kind – in my case Springsteen never fails. *Badlands* has been instrumental in finishing most of my favourites, but equally has done a painting in. Either way, it gets it off the fence. If I'm navigating the early stages with a less than convincing sense of where I'm going I will let Spotify do its thing. Or iPlay uplifting radio shows to order – some Dermot O'Leary Wexford wit and wisdom always helps to lighten a painting funk when I'm in one. And equally to celebrate when I'm out of it. Tailor your companions appropriately and accordingly. And if things are a little rocky in

your head, and by extension in your art, I suggest you go all in with the solid dance tunes; there is very little that some George Michael's 'Freedom' maxed up can't cure.

I'm in good company here. A lady sitter to John Singer Sargent regaled how he was battling hard and unsuccessfully with her portrait. Hitting despair at his efforts around her opals, he stepped away to the piano and 'thumped out the bass of a Fauré duet' with the sitter's husband! He then leapt back to the canvas completing the opals in some swift masterly strokes, the one artistic expression apparently releasing the block and stimulating the breakthrough in his brain. How wonderful. The painter Kandinsky compared colours on a palette to the keys of a piano and even likened the human soul to the piano itself. He felt that as an artist used a palette, it was in effect playing different musical notes, causing 'vibrations in the soul'. My primal need for music when painting may not be totally left-field eccentric after all.

Working in isolation, I also love the feeling of being connected in some way to other people which is why I switch up my day between my own tunes and (my now studio family of) Radio 2. Sometimes I need to plug in and to feel part of something bigger; it is reassuring and soothing and a reminder of being part of the whole. Music has the ability to bring us both somewhere beyond ourselves altogether, and also all together there. Be it the transcending collective electricity of Freddie Mercury's slam dunk at Live Aid or a singsong around our kitchen table at home, music is a glorious energy in motion, and I always want to tap some of that.

Having said all of that, I do know that not all art, and certainly not all artists, welcome music as a backdrop. Some, such as a writer pal of mine, demand perfect silence. But when she needs to remove herself from her craft, to let a plot or a turn of phrase marinate, she turns to her piano, safe in the knowledge that flooding her active brain with music will somehow soften the chaos going on in the artistic lobe.

A few years back I was obviously on a musical positivity roll. Not being a great recogniser of a familiar face, I found myself at a party, encouraging a lovely gentleman, called Mike, in his musical endeavours. I said that I thought it was wonderful he played the guitar – how 'therapeutic' I suggested to this bemused man on my right – singer, songwriter and co-founder of Genesis. I might have even mentioned 'so does my Mum…'

6. **Get a bit selfish**: Now not to be rude, but are you a people pleaser? You see, just sometimes – and I don't want to encourage you to be a less than gorgeous person, but … we need to be that bit selfish to give to our wellbeing and creativity what they require. I know this isn't how you were brought up, but hear me out.

There are times when I have to downright lie as to my whereabouts in order not to cry with frustration when I have a superb exhibition going on in my head and not enough hours to get it onto canvas. As a Creative, you're generally thought of as unfettered by banalities of time frames and routine, painting away the witching hours in a cloud of absinthe and slumbering by day on a red velvet sofa. It's true enough, for many, that time spent in creativity is indeed a break from reality, but when it is your very real reality the truth is somewhat different. Carving out your career is tough emotionally (some days, boy oh boy), existentially (yes it IS that important) and financially (it may not buy happiness but it buys decent coffee), and I have a deep-seated tenacity when I'm on a roll to keep on rollin'.

There are even chapters when dedication flips from pastime

or vocation to clear-cut obsession. Don't beat yourself up too much about being selfish – occasionally. In these times I fail miserably to be a half decent friend, but as long as it's not your permanent default (watch out for this!) you can make amends down the line.

Psychologists have now identified a 'switch cost' which recognises a performance dip where a change in task/attention is required – it's not selfish, it's science. Be unapologetic about the time you need to carve out to give to your creativity what it asks of you. Have the confidence and belief in your work to say no to people to protect the time and energy you require to fulfil what you need to do. I see it as 'good' selfish. Your energy is finite so you need to use it wisely. A great girlfriend used to make me repeat '*never apologise … never explain*'. She is kind and brilliant beyond words and makes a difference in so many people's lives (thank you Rachel), but she knows the vital necessity of prioritising in order to get it done. Your work IS IMPORTANT. And people will respect it if you will.

And here's the thing – when you show this respect to your work it will respond and reward you in multiple kind. Dedicate time to your creative calling – it really, really matters.

Top Tip: If you find they're still not getting your visceral need to hunker down, bore them out of your life (selfish *and* boring – what a catch!). Go into infinitesimal detail on how you can't make lunch as you're battling with grey tones in your greyscape, in your deepest greyest voice, and soon they won't want to hang out with you anyway. Job done.

7. **Get moving**: Firstly – exercise … seriously. You shake a leg and get that air into your lungs, thereafter you sleep, therefore you

sparkle. Plus our old joints need it. What sort of exercise and how much is up to you but have it in your game plan. It's totally unsatisfactory to be a great creator if you're dead. Your benefactors may disagree but be selfish – stick around.

Secondly – get moving in your work. The feeling of growth and a sense of progress in a particular work or in your work as a whole, are deeply satisfying and make the testing times worthwhile. It puts more petrol in the tank, and refuels you going forward. Have a routine in how you approach your craft but sometimes go rogue and claim a plot twist – your work needs the freshness, the raw emotion, the zing. We have to have routine in our creativity but we also have to set it aside and go be crazy just once in a while.

Thirdly – from time to time move around. Physically, geographically, literally – see beyond your everyday vista to keep your attitude and powers of perception fresh. The actress Joanna Lumley suggests we all buy an atlas and keep it by the bed and '*remember you can go anywhere*'. Absolutely fabulous. The artist's bank account may not lend itself to regular jet-setting but it's the free mind and the dream spinning that I adore. Sometimes, I beg of you, pack your bag and hit the road for an injection of energy and inspiration. If travelling solo it can be daunting at first, but it's one of the most liberating experiences you can have. Who knows too what wonderful people and ideas you'll encounter, not to mention the confidence it gives you when you've ventured out there alone. For me it shakes things up when I need it and gives me perspective on my work and on my life. Use your time on the open road to crystallise what it is you want to achieve, on all frontiers going forward, when you journey back to home sweet home.

8. **Make an effort**: On the days you feel least like it, make most effort. Wear wanton red or Hermes orange or a slash of hot pink – if only to go buy some hummus. If you haven't woken up feeling totally exquisite, or even vaguely human, act your way out of it. Never leave the house in your pyjamas. No. Not ever. I have recently decided to step through the front door in the mornings presuming I look much more attractive than I actually do (my eyes increasingly reveal fewer of the riveting details), it makes for a far better day.

9. **Make a date**: Don't shoot the messenger, but a thought … If you're single, and don't quite wish to be, consider taking in some life re-affirming dating. Which then raises the question: to date a fellow Creative? The optimum tango or two peacocks together? Or perhaps entwining with a more earthy practical pair of hands who can rescue you in ways that matter and re-ground you when needs be? My jury is out. I won't be giving any dating advice to anyone, only to say swim with the fishies but watch out for the sharks. There may be tears. There may be tequila. But there's ALWAYS potential (and a reassuring midnight cheese toastie should you have endured a testing encounter with a frog or a cod).

Whatever the state of your romantic affairs, the state of your mental affairs is, frankly, crucial. For your creativity to be both productive and rewarding you need to get some good mind managing moves in your armoury. Think of them as taking vitamins for optimum balance and to keep you hitting your best in your game …

Chapter 5

MIND MATTERS

'There are always flowers for those who want to see them.'

— Henri Matisse —
Painter

The Creative's mind can be a confusing place to be at times. It can be as fragile as it can be brilliant, and there are times when it might benefit from some attention to keep it at its most promising.

As Creatives we are bringing something into being that hasn't been there before. Generally it doesn't just happen with a 'whoosh' or a 'tah dah', but you've much more chance of that happening if you are in the right headspace to begin. And to continue as such each day.

As you get going you will naturally begin to show your creative work to audiences beyond your own desk and daydreams. And when it comes to properly revealing our creativity to the world we must keep ourselves healthy and our thought processes on an even keel. It feels both terrifying and exciting – this revealing business – and setting the scene for your best work to happen, and keep happening, is vital.

You may have your own thoughts around this. (You will – you are a Creative!) Here are mine:

1. **Know yourself!**: Be viscerally aware of your strengths and your weaknesses and always play to the former (larks vs. owls is a basic, save the more demanding aspects for when you're most awake). We all have chinks in our creative armour – triggers that will have you performing at less than your brilliant best. You might be prone to procrastination (set a schedule) or easily distracted (disable all pings), or have a propensity to give up rather than work through (a Mars bar per designated word count?). You'll know your culprits and your cures. Recognise them and formulate your practice to make your days as productive as possible – keep that one step ahead.

2. **Reset your vibe**: If you need to up your energy or shake off some cobwebs, as Nike says: 'Just Do It'. You can start over anytime. Each morning. Change your story! Pretend it's your birthday. Eat some cake. Hug a tree. Touch your talisman. Flirt with the barista. Do whatever you have to do. Get the mind-frame the best it can. Basically, set your day in motion with high artistic aspirations. Crazy not to. Turn up in anticipation of divine inspiration, or at the very least intervention when you're about to send your work over a cliff. And then open yourself to the flow.

3. **Spread the love**: Every day I set up with three or four works on the go. That way I'm in with a betting chance that one of them at the very least will be sympathetic to my intentions. (Extraordinarily Monet apparently had up to 80 when he was doing his Thames studies – how on earth?) I find if I'm working on a few at the same time advancement in one can inform the other. It's as if they pull each other along – a breakthrough in one can be a key in the next.... I rotate throughout the week to determine which one gets the primetime productive slot – for

me the 8.30 am to 10.45 am window is when the high-octane action happens, riding on a caffeine high before elevenses' over-analysis creeps in. However if I then find that something is really working and on a roll I'll stay ploughing that furrow for longer.

Whilst the 'musical canvases' methodology I use may be entirely impractical to the way you work, I find it means that I always have hope. (My Dad taught me about all things hope in life. Keep it, please, forever in your toolkit too.) For me working on more than one thing at a time keeps me in the positive place I need to be. At least one will be working, maybe two, possibly three. If all your creative buds don't blossom, remember Lucian Freud actually hired someone for the purpose of destroying failed canvases. Some are destined for greatness, some not so much. Songwriters might average out one good in five, or maybe one in ten. Though if you're Coldplay's Chris Martin I think every day's probably a bullseye. (I'd love to know…).

When your creativity is flowing it makes your soul sing in a way that very little else does. You get into your rhythm and you're in sync. When you're working in that vibration GOOD THINGS HAPPEN. The energy you're getting from the good thing happening transmutes into the energy you need to lift the next baby to its full potential. When you feel good about your art and about yourself – good art happens.

This way of working might of course not be appropriate to your particular medium; a novelist, for instance, is unlikely to have more than one novel on the go. In such cases, it's helpful – so I'm told – to have some other exercise in your medium to hand – the novelist might have a blog, or write a letter, or be lucky enough to do the occasional magazine article to alternate routine without breaking focus on the opus in hand.

4. **Keep the wheels oiled and rolling**: You want your creativity to be second nature so that there is no divide between it and you – you are all of one. Indeed it reflects the deepest parts of you, parts that sometimes you don't even know are there. You want to be able to pick up your expressions where you left off (like great friends do). This takes a certain investment in the relationship so that no awkwardness pops up between you. Writers know that reading – devouring words of all different flavours – is the best kale smoothie they can put into their output. And writing even a few words daily helps you stay in the flow. My dear writer friend Jess suggests 'touching your book every day' – just checking in to keep your head in the game and so it knows you're still there. That way, the whirling processes of the subconscious will keep working away in the background in the hours between. Mr Garbett pleaded with us, whilst all other subjects were getting due revision for the Leaving Cert, to fit in ten minutes doodling each day to keep the right muscles flexed and channels open to up the flow. On the phone or waiting for the pizza to heat, to put pen/pencil/glitter marker to paper and take it for a walk. I'm certain it pulled us doodlers up a grade or two when our performance counted. Keep the wheels turning and you will feel the benefits in your flow after multiple doodle days. Scribble, strum, shimmy or hum – as pertinent to your sphere – what important friend isn't worth ten minutes of your day?

5. **Don't put pressure on the process**: Commit to the here and now of what you're doing, with full focus and confidence in what you know, and then see where it takes you. Yes, absolutely have the intention of where you are going hovering over you constantly and consistently as you work, but don't be singularly (or neurotically) attached to the specifics of the outcome. '*The painting has a life*

of its own. I try to let it come through'. How much do I love the faith that Jackson Pollock had in the divine creative force? The cutting-edge abstract impressionist painter apparently considered himself as only a 'helpful bystander'. This non-attachment to outcome is a really worthy ingredient in your creative kitchen. I was lucky to train in early days in the atelier of Lavender Hill Studios (now London Fine Art Studios). Anne, my clever tutor, would say '*commit to a line, but be sympathetic to change*'. Vision, yes wonderful; over-attachment to how it must turn out, a creativity killer.

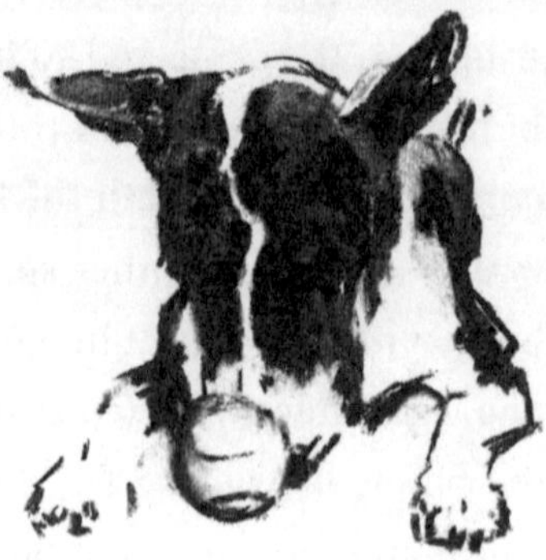

Be open, too, to happy accidents. Inadvertently, a 'mismove' can make all the difference in pushing your good to great. Sometimes the best thing you can do is welcome these shiny curveballs in.

Remember to focus on the process itself and enjoy it if you can, as this will manifest in your work. Some will know that this is less easy with commissions and deadlines – my idea of a nightmare. Generally, for a fee the subject matter needs to be recognisable; add to this the high expectations and acceptable time frames, and I can find these particular pressures crippling. Unfulfilled deadlines make me cry. But when I can work in that vibe of enthusiasm or joy for what I am doing, my brushwork is stronger and my colourways sing. It's a feeling of working in alignment with my soul, and when it is actually coming together it's the closest thing to grace that I know.

6. **Don't put pressure on your art**: Really, it's not fair on the art. When you go on a date it's so much better to go not actually expecting to meet 'THE ONE'. Doing so sets the bar too high – it's only going to disappoint. Instead see the encounter as an opportunity to enjoy yourself and who knows where it might go! This is the approach you need to bring to your creativity, especially if you've been struggling. Just turn up with the expectation of having a joyful encounter (whilst of course putting in the effort, just in case it is THE ONE). Maintain your standards but don't be single-minded about it manifesting into a great 'work' or a 'piece'. Very few could fulfil a brief to write a bestselling Man Booker Prize winner or a hit record on demand. Creatives are tender creatures. Instead let the music come, keep it rock'n'roll and see how it grows. Don't criticise it – critique it yes, this is constructive – but you and your art are both on the same side here.

   Develop that respect for your work as a whole so your maternal/paternal instinct kicks in. When preparing for a launch, an exhibition or an opening night, if you hit gridlock or breakdown mode, it's totally not fair on your endgame and your bigger goals. I see my paintings as my babies and send them off out into the world with the best start I can give them in anticipation of a welcoming forever home.

7. **Recalibrate**: When panic sets in, normalise it. This is an ugly duckling moment – that's all. Take out the negative filter that panic brings in between you and your work and connect with your subject again. Don't build barriers – re-centre and pause.

Take a moment or two. Breathe. Switch back to positive. '*You think I can't do this? Hah – just watch!*' And as you were …

8. **Recaffeinate** … if it helps.

9. **Stay high**: If mid-session it's feeling 'hit and miss', keep going until it's a 'hit'. Even a mini one. It may seem counterintuitive but if I down tools for too long when on a low, I find that they're mighty heavy to pick back up. So if you want to step away to regain clarity on return, absolutely do. Generally, however, to keep a steady energy I take breaks in my work when it's all going well; a highlight that sings, a lost edge that's pleasing, brush down and kettle on. Then I return with an oomph which is distinctly not dread, and that upwards oomph in attitude makes all the difference for me.

   Ernest Hemingway's advice on the psychology of the writing process was to not '*pump yourself dry*'. Instead stop in a place that leaves the right energy for the following day: '*when you're still going good and you come to an interesting place and you know what's going to happen next*'. Then step away and let the subconscious mind do the work. To be resumed … with enthusiasm, once more.

10. **Switch it up and see it differently**: When you can no longer see your work objectively you need to look at it once removed, more 'in abstract'. The celebrated author Zadie Smith recommends that writers try reading their own work as a stranger would read it, or better, as an enemy might (ouch). If it's a visual work of art, turn it upside down on the easel or look at its reflection in a mirror, or even once removed through a camera lens. You'll see it afresh and mistakes will make themselves all too clearly apparent

to you. Over-familiarity can lead us to have selective powers of perception. Sometimes you need to step away for a while. I keep the paintings I'm working on facing the wall between sessions so as not to get over accustomed to them. The weaknesses then pop out in cheekily stark relief when I say hello to them once more.

11. **Back to the nursery slopes**: In the off-kilter moments (less than a block, more than a lazy mood), I swap to something I'm fairly confident in accomplishing and that I can't really screw up – the easier stuff that requires application but not necessarily pzazz. If your Muse is MIA get on with more earthy endeavours: fact checking, ordering supplies, stretching a canvas, polishing your Stradivarius, that sort of thing. Onwards and, ok perhaps a little sideways, but it's still some sense of progress which, for me, is key.

12. **Back to the bar**: If it's seriously not happening and you're finding yourself a liability in your own studio, just accept you're having a non-art rubbish day, write it off workwise and do something in another direction. Hoover? Go to an exhibition? Make falafels? Do anything to break the routine. If you're doing more harm than good and failing to express yourself in any respectable manner at all, by all means say to heck with being a super-creator (just for today) and pour yourself that G & T instead.

13. **A train for thoughts!**: Sometimes for no good reason a funk will just 'appear'. And no matter what we do, we just can't seem to halt negative thoughts from whirling about in our brains. It's not so much a block as mental obstacles we're placing in our own paths. According to the National Science Foundation we average 12,000 to 60,000 thoughts a day, an overwhelming majority of which are estimated to be negative, with 95 per cent being exactly

the same repetitive thoughts as the day before. How exhausting. Cue the Queen of Positivity, the inspirational Louise Hay: '*You are not a helpless victim of your own thoughts but rather a master of your mind.*' Right so – time for some mastery. My always inspiring friend Dee shared an antidote visualisation technique with me. If there's a particular something playing on your mind like a woodpecker and you have given it due consideration and done your best to solve it, but it persists to pester, she advises as follows:

Stand on an imaginary station platform seeing the train arrive and when the carriage doors open, pile the 'trouble' onto the train, doors close, and watch it leaving the station. Still there? Again, onto the next train until that too leaves the station. And again, on repeat, until that pesky problem is firmly in Cockfosters or beyond.

We in the arts each have our own techniques for managing our minds and evolving our processes. What follows next may speak more to your inner flower child than inner fugue, but they are practices which work for many and have worked for me. Some may resonate, others may just irritate. Any kookiness is by no means a prerequisite to being a great Creative, but is an integral part of the creative 'trip' for some.

Chapter 6

FIND THE GAP

'Nothing truly new and creative can come into this world except through that gap, that clear space of infinite possibility.'

— Eckhart Tolle —
Spiritual Teacher and Author

'MIND THE GAP': I used to hear it every morning on my way to my city office – rushing below London, in constant Stressville, anywhere but present. Now I mind the gap, happily, in the peace of my studio but it's a better gap, a welcome gap, and one in which on a very good day, hopefully the magic begins.

This promising gap I refer to is the silent space between our thoughts – the centre point of our stillness. We speak of being true, well there is nowhere truer for any of us. The seeds, sparks and hunches that we get in this still place tend to be just what we, and by extension what our work, needs at that moment in time. Arriving there is rarely not worth making the effort of getting there. Paradoxically, what we're striving for is the point where all effort – all action, and the constant buzz with us – ceases.

I appreciate that the concept of stillness within, and the practices of seeing it out, might not be everyone's cup of camomile tea. You might consider yourself to be a dedicated builder's-with-a-splash-of-milk. But remember how we spoke of opening yourself up to new possibilities? Not even embracing – just listening. Or in this case reading eight short pages. G'wan, I dare you.

The Mechanics

It all starts under the simple umbrella of meditation. Don't run away! It's truly fabulous stuff. You get to take a holiday, every day, for as long as you want, from your own life. And if you love your life and don't need a holiday from it – lucky you – you get to take a short break which will make your creative life even better. Happy days.

Still Meditation: Meditation at its essence is very simple, and I find it's best to keep it that way. Some people use mantras; others prefer not to, finding that they can trigger thoughts which confuse. I find it easier just to follow the flow of my breathing. All it entails is just being in the present moment, with yourself, and letting yourself just be. That's it. To begin, settle down somewhere peaceful and clock where you're at. Tune into your surrounds and take note of your body within that space. If you are outside take a moment to drink in the sky above and the earth below. Tune into the sounds and the smells. Rest your hands gently on your knees: facing upwards as an invitation to receive, or downwards if you want to ground. Gather your perceptions to right here, right now. A recognition of a heartbeat. Notice where your limbs are resting and acknowledge your own rhythms as you relax. Begin to become aware of your breathing, follow your natural breath, in and out. As you continue, thoughts might gatecrash. This is natural and no problem. Just let them come and go. Don't try to suppress them, just don't give them any airtime. Your mind might continue to wander again (of course it will – we're incessant adventurers!). When so, just notice that it has wandered and bring it gently back to the wave of your breath. Always back to the breath.

As your mind settles and noise and thoughts recede, your deeper consciousness will start to deliver up what you need to know. It might tell you what you need to do or divulge the detail that escaped you earlier and you'd since left to one side. It may throw up words or resolutions that were previously beyond reach or plant the plot bridge that your character needs. Give your mind time and you will eventually find a gut instinct, a sense of clarity or just a peaceful sense of knowing.

This is often for me a key to unlocking a painting. It gives me a gentle push out of a bunker if I've been stuck there, or a solution to something I couldn't figure out. Sometimes the answer doesn't present itself fully there and then, but there will be a moment, perhaps later in the day or night, when I will suddenly know. Only recently I had a startling 3am awakening to the words 'cerulean blue'. REM, or zen-induced I'm not sure which, but it just dropped in when I was at my most relaxed and it was totally what my spaniel's coat was waiting for.

Moving Meditation: Meditating doesn't have to confine you to your lotus position (or your kitchen chair). Moving forms of meditation might be more your thing and keep you zoning in on a longer basis. Some swear by Qigong and Tai Chi; equally brilliant is just mindfully walking through nature, or swimming in a river or in the sea. In fact anything in nature when done mindfully is a valuable meditation. The most popular, by a country mile, for those interested in moving while they mindfully breathe, is yoga.

Yoga is not all about creating Instagram opportunities for the goddesses of unattainable bendiness (ok, not *necessarily*) but landing these creaking bones onto the mat is high on my rescue and maintenance list.

I myself am more like an awkward pigeon. Some years ago a lovely Long Island yogi told me I was 'always going to be the (pigeon) chick with the tight hamstrings'. Maddeningly she was spot on. This makes for a dicey downward dog and fewer pretzel poses but it doesn't lessen the benefits one bit.

Painting for me is standing and walking all day to and from my easel between strokes, and a sort of cock-eared slanting to the left stance with my right hand up is how I currently spend most waking hours. Firstly, and practically, yoga straightens me out. Secondly, it's relaxing (my best pose is Savasana – the bit where you get to sleep at the end). Thirdly, yoga does wonders for the spine, both actually and metaphysically. With a stronger backbone we are predisposed to carry life's baggage with much greater ease. Finally, and vitally, by creating spaces in the body it creates an important space elsewhere. Space where, sometimes, the really good stuff comes into land.

You know your yoga practice is worth the effort when the space you create while on the mat remains with you when you are off. When I'm in the swing of a regular practice it yields an internal refuge I can call upon when I need equilibrium and balance. Music to a Creative's off-kilter ears. (If you want a gem of a teacher in your life I am sharing with you the treasure that is www.nicolecroftyoga.com. She's amazing.)

If you're not ready for, or up for, a formal practice, even bringing the following into your life will reap immediate benefits to your headspace:

Mini-barely-there-at-all Meditation: Aka engaging 'present moment awareness'. For everyone this is important, on both the good days and the bad. When you arrive at your desk/easel/ballet barre be sure too that you've arrived at yourself. Your energy in the kick-off sets your tone for the session. It needs to be positive and it needs to be focused – when you have multiple mind channels playing at once, as I tend to, you may need to reign it in. Your job, as a Creative, is to turn up, *all of you*, with the most positive mindset you can muster, open yourself to the process, and see where the journey takes you. At the very least take a minute or two just to tune into what you are doing, hone your attention, gather your intentions and just BE. HERE. NOW.

It comes down to mindfulness. Even the sound of the word for me is delicious and sumptuous and promising, if a teeny bit confusing. It's really more a place of 'neutralness', letting go of the distractions that prevent us being in the here and now rather than the active filling of our mind space. It allows for the falling away, not only of stresses and distractions, but of the barriers we build between us and the moment (full of potential) we are in.

The Deeper Stuff

About that potential – mind-body wellness guru, Deepak Chopra, advocates that the mechanics of achieving our full potential come down to two qualities within our consciousness: attention and intention. By forming an 'intention' on the object of our 'attention', over time it will become apparent how to direct our energies to get there and reach the outcomes we desire. See? It's totally doable.

Here's How: Place your attention towards what you want for your creativity, and have the intention, or even a sankalpa (yes it's a thing, keep reading), to see it through.

The yogis will always begin their practice with a 'sankalpa' which is Sanskrit for resolve or intention. Think of bringing this extra kick to your cosmic cocktail. Your inner shot of tequila. It can be a short-term goal or value when it comes to creativity (or creative endeavour). But go the whole hog while you're at it and set a long-term aspiration in terms of where you want to go. Having an intention is simply like having a road map, which is helpful no matter what the journey. Try to plot yours, not just for your current session or creative focus today, but for the longer term. Heck, think big.

Being a Creative is a stayer's race, not a sprint. Regularly honing your attention will reset your GPS for the bigger picture. Tune in fresh each session/week/work, forgiving yourself the hiccups, dead ends and wipe-outs that have gone before. Acknowledge instead all your incremental steps towards your long-term worthy vision and creative goals. Then eyes ahead.

The Kookier Stuff

A mindful practice will lead you to more intuitive productivity in your artform. And when we start working from a more intuitive place, magic can begin to happen.

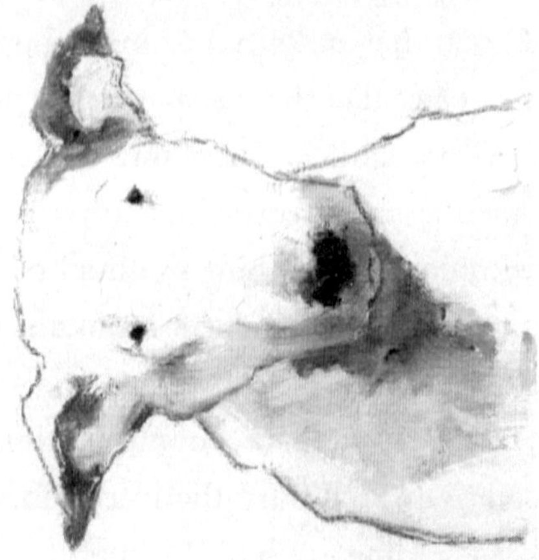

Deepak (yes, we're on first name terms here) has had much to do with bringing mindful thinking mainstream. His bookshelf best teaches that when we learn to live from the level of the soul, it helps our fear and anxiety to fall away and to appreciate the potential of the moment instead.

When I first started painting I would listen to his guided meditations in my ear pods as a melodic uplifting start to my studio day. His book *Synchrodestiny* was a favourite early read and it might be one for you too.

Serendipity: (How much do I love this word?!) '*The art of tripping upon pleasure*'. 'Serendipity' is an older and simpler cousin to Carl Jung's concept of 'synchronicity', and Deepak's book '*Synchrodestiny*' is the bridge between the two. In it he writes of coincidences appearing in our lives as messages about the miraculous potential of each moment – as Creatives we must love this.

Fresh from reading this very book, I decided it was time to shake things up a little. (I'm inclined to such shake-ups; while they occasionally prove to be disastrous, sometimes they're rather fabulous). The Sunday night movie '*The Holiday*' had Kate Winslet and Cameron Diaz, fed up with their mildly tragic existences (hello!) on opposite sides of the Atlantic, get online, and within minutes a house swap was in the works. Adventures ahoy – I thought I could use some of that. I typed in: 'my London for your New York', and by Thursday, I was off.

Now I recognise a mid-life crisis when I look it in the eye and see clearly and fully the hallmarks of a 40-something deranged divorcee (hands up – I was, but that's not all I was!) No, this was none of the above, but the best thing I ever did.

First morning in the Big Apple – up with the dawn, sneakers on, I walked from Soho to Lower Manhattan and back up to Midtown by midday. I went into a church to thank 'them upstairs' as all felt just right in my heart. Something, at last, had changed. It felt like the lights had been switched back on. I felt a sense of peace I hadn't known in years. I picked up a coffee and sat with my eyes closed in the sun, in Madison Square. I felt, well, alive, and blessed with grace. I have known that feeling to be all encompassing twice in my life. The first time was when I put the final stroke on a painting which was to later be a brave musketeer for me out in the wider world; my first painting to be published in a beautiful book, surrounded by all my painting heroes, living and left. I knew at that final brushstroke in painting him that something big was shifting, and I knew I could actually paint. And here at this moment now, sitting on my bench, the same feeling in my every cell, for no spectacular reason, no tangible cause at all.

I upped to go, the whole of 5th Avenue to cruise. I heard Deepak's voice and naturally went to turn my iPod off. No iPod. I realised then it was Deepak's voice, right there, chatting away beside me. Confirmed in an instant by his crystal-armed signature spectacles. This voice that had been a soothing uplift in my recent dark days, encouraging me to trust in life's path (and to notice coincidences!), was here beside me counselling a very tall man who was leaning in to listen. I had even checked if he might be giving any lectures in NYC that week, but he was meant to be in California. His words I overheard as we exited the gate together: '*So keep it simple, really, just trust in the bigger picture, it WILL all work out, trust is the answer, every time*'.

I will, I do, and yes I truly believe it is.

Namaste

x

Meditation low down - just so you know...

It's not difficult.

You don't need to stop your thoughts, just find the gaps between them.

Even noticing you have thoughts is mighty progress (hello your silent witness).

The way to quieten your mind is not to force it or command it but to gently, non-judgementally, watch it.

In meditation our body produces fewer stress hormones and other chemicals that speed up the ageing process – Yaaay – save on Botox™

Even a few minutes makes a difference. You may not witness a choir of angels, but the real benefits are what happen for you in the other hours of the day. (A small hum of one angel, perhaps.)

It is a straightforward and simple way of reconnecting with your core self and making good decisions from there.

At the bare minimum of the bonus scale – being more centred helps us to respond to, instead of reacting to, life and all its baggage as it heaps up at your door. This can only be a good thing on this crazy rollercoaster …

Aren't I right?

SECTION III: TAKE COVER

I'm not going to sugar coat it – this creativity business can be tough. This section is written for the hard days we can face and the bleakness that can descend into our feel-good art party.

Each of us in our own way is putting forth a part of ourselves, in the face of – horror! – others' opinions and the world at large. To be vulnerable is part and parcel of the Creative's lot. It is an inherent cost which is damning three-fold: it cannot be avoided; it's part of the process of being a Creative and – this might be the worst element of it – it's necessary. Much as we might not like it, it helps us to grow, to thrive, to evolve to be who we authentically are, and to hit our higher ground. Vulnerability is at the very heart of the Creative and the trade-off for any discomfort is generally worth it. Darn it. It's a 'good cost', if you will.

Common in the Creative's lot lurk other 'costs' however, which can, quite frankly, make us want to hide. You may already know something of blocks and black holes of depression which tear at our souls and undermine our very selves, and which threaten our art (and our relationships and even our bank balances). Hard hats at the ready for **Chapters 7** and **8** respectively. The only upside is that they are not usually ongoing states of being and – believe me on this – they can be overcome.

Chapter 7

THE BLOCK

'Try not to resist the changes that come your way. Instead let life live through you. And do not worry that your life is turning upside down. How do you know that the side you are used to is better than the one to come?'

— Rumi —
Poet and Spiritual Master

Ok. So you've got a block. Firstly, don't keep hurling yourself against the wall – I've tried that, it isn't pretty. This wall is no platform 9¾ and you'll only end up in A&E. Instead, gather your fortitude and either blow a hole in that darned wall, or find a ladder and climb over it.

Being weary of attitude and dreary of strokes is one thing – but the dreaded block, another. Many will regard it as a normal part of the creative process – almost an inevitability. Some will mistake burn-out for a block (Creatives – you can't run on empty). Others will say there's no such thing as creative block. Maddeningly I know there is, but I try to see it as a wake-up call for growth.

A real creative block, it seems to me, is part and parcel of cripplingly uncomfortable – but wholly necessary – change. It often comes when you're not satisfied where you're at artistically yet can't visualise where you're going. And it can be really mentally challenging.

If things aren't working – I mean really NOT WORKING – we need to (wo)man up and face it. I have come to believe (admittedly quite a few skins later) that blocks are usually times where you're shedding your old outdated skin, to allow for the new. We can't remain static, and anyway, who wants to? Try to use a time of block to work on letting go of attachments to old ways that don't serve you any longer. These may be in your routine, your techniques, your vision for your work, or your tastes as they change. Then look to move forward with a new true sense of self.

It's not easy. Hitting a block can envelop you as fully as a love affair going off the tracks. It can make you feel that this art, into which you've poured so much of your very being – which is in fact *part of* your very being – is betraying you. Please trust that it's not. There are simply times when we need to look deep within to unlock the patterns we have tied ourselves into, to free and better our evolving selves going forward.

In times of crisis what we need is not headbanging or poor-me-ing. What we need is a strategy.

Emergency Step 1: Give yourself a break. Pour your favourite brew, light the fire and hunker down with an emergency A-Team of books by brilliant teachers. Be kind to yourself. Criticising your efforts here is cruel and unproductive, so have a cry and then set your compass for their inspiring writings. My go-tos (and I believe Amazon do emergency deliveries) are listed in recovery priority order below:

Julia Cameron – *The Artist's Way* (for when you need the crash team in)
Elizabeth Gilbert – *Big Magic* (for all things creative inspiration, resuscitation and faith restored)

Eckhart Tolle – *The Power of Now* (the soul stuff)
Tony Bates – *Depression: The Common Sense Approach* (the low stuff)
Eileen Caddy – *Opening Doors Within* (just a beautiful way to start the day)
TED Talks – when you can read no more, immerse and emerge refocused (I know you will find solace for starters with the brilliant Brené Brown).

And specifically for painters:

Robert Henri – *The Art Spirit* (in remission – the feel-good factor and painting pearls of wisdom)
Richard Schmid – *Alla Prima – Everything I Know About Painting* (for the painting constructs and technical know-how, and all-round warm-hearted TLC).

Emergency Step 2: Remove yourself from your own head when it's getting fragile up there. Sometimes I'm just seeing it all askew, or not at all, and need a break from my endless conversations with me. Cross referring you back to getting yourself in the now (Chapter 6), although at these most testing of times I want to be anywhere else. A bit of simple meditative practice to empty your head of thoughts can be a real help here.

Emergency Step 3: When it's all gone Pete Tong, remove yourself from the crash site and go back to who and what inspires you. Re-find your inspiration, re-find your spirit within. There is always a way. Take yourself to your 'soul spot', metaphorically and physically, where your instincts and your muses collide.

- **Go to your Greats**: I think this can really help. Playwriters amongst you – sign up for the matinee and the evening performance, all week long. Haunt the stage door if you must.

Sculptors, a humble suggestion – if the piggybank would allow: a daytrip to Paris – if only because we should all do it in the name of romance, even on our own, even once. Go bask in the ambience of the Rodins, Claudels, Maillots and Degas, and take in the Musée d'Orsay (it would be a little bit rude to the creative gods not to). And if the bank balance or small children or tight schedule won't allow, equally perfect is a trip to your capital city wherever you are. So many beautiful statues and monuments are majestically residing on our very own streets to be enjoyed and studied for not a penny from your purse. Musicians – go high-brow to the concert hall or funk it up at Glastonbury. Dancers, does Covent Garden call? Pattern cutters and fashionistas – get to the design collections you adore and back to the revolutionaries with you. Visit the V&A in London – Alexander McQueen, Chanel and all things vintage couture, a smorgasbord of fashion highs, breathe in their creative oxygen; or at the very least consume your best back copies of Vogue. Or wherever and whatever touchstone works for you. Think TIMELESS, classic, all time goodies – those who shook off the shackles of *their* time and traditions – you get the picture. Writers, down quills and read your inquisitive hearts out. If you can get to London, a day, afternoon, or even an hour in the British Library will remind you why you do (and love) what you do. Painters amongst you, stand in front of your favourite painting in any way possible. William Orpen turned keys for me in the National Gallery of Ireland – make merry to Merrion Square. The National Portrait Gallery is my panacea in London, the Met is my shrine in New York (don't I sound terribly glam??)

But seriously – it works. Something in me changed when I met the painting 'The Royal Court Theatre Directors' by Justin Mortimer. I was drawn in by its composition in a way that I wanted to physically get into that painting, to be part of it and find out what was going on. I found it compelling. It was beyond aesthetically pleasing; it required something of me and I wanted to be involved. It kick-started something deep within me that's been buzzing ever since.

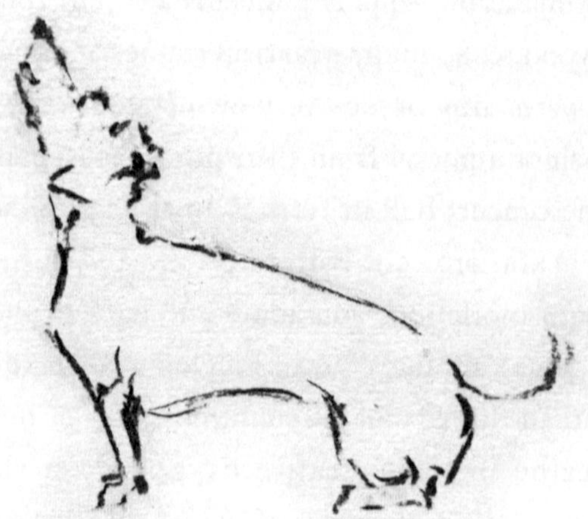

Whatever your art – go to the very centre of it. Remember what it was which first engulfed and impassioned you – whether a book or a score or the anti-heroine's 32 fouettés in *Swan Lake* – and immerse yourself right in it. Go back to the very beginning and be humbled again, by what once humbled you before.

Deep in the trenches during a near fatal block I ended up having one of the most beautiful days of my life. Again up with the dawn on a late spring day in London, I went for a walk with my 'I mean business' trainers on. I headed across the city to make my way back through the passages of tone and tempera and time. I needed the misty Tate Turners, the shimmering uplift of a Klimt and to breathe in a Whistler to get my own struggling efforts out of my head. '*Nocturne in Blue and Gold*' – his painting of the old Battersea bridge where I walked after work every day. I learned his constructs – a lead white oil ground overlaid with a palette of lead white and lamp black with prussian blue. It settled me and brought me back to where I wanted to go, with a distinct glimmer of hope lighting the pathway ahead.

Learn from the Greats in your specific creative fields what you can. Try to understand their own building blocks and their processes. When in the presence of beauty, breathe it in. Work out what speaks to you? And why? Bring your notebook or your camera (if permitted) to record and to crystallise thereafter. I find it impossible to remember all the details that tickle me unless I note them somehow. (You should keep a notebook, whatever your art – if not for this moment in time – you never know what might fit into another ballad/composition/collection one day. Log all details, ideas, thoughts and inspirations that nuzzle you, and especially those that make you doubletake!)

And once again, jump disciplines; it's the same creative spirit underpinning all our arts. The highly creative (and spirited!) Bloomsbury Group continuously embroider the catwalks – even the marbled paper that once bound their literature has been translated into fashion-house Fendi's fabric techniques!

Cross-pollinate all the way. You may find you need to tune into a different musical instrument to unlock the struggle with your own. You might need to go beyond your own artistry's playing field completely. When you step outside, inspiration can pop in through the cat flap waiting for you to come home as if it was there all along. If a heavy metal rock gig is going to unlock the simile in your sonnet – that's divine.

- **Go to your kitchen**: If others' genius isn't pushing the right buttons you might find that magic lies in the mundane. My very favourite comedy sketch is Michael McIntyre's conversation amongst the condiments of his kitchen cupboard. Hilariously, joyfully, creatively spun from the utterly everyday ordinary – it is comedic writing gold. Sometimes our muse is kicking back much closer to home, right in front of our nose, somewhere to the left of the kettle.

- **Go back to your nature**: You might just need to get out your front door into the natural world around you. David Hockney went to the forests, John Denver the mountains, Bowie went to Mars. The poppy fields drew Monet and then he drew them right back. If it is beckoning, get yourself to the coast to breathe in the salt and the sea and the sand. But you might also find nature in the dank of a puddle or the riotous beauty of a candy pink peony in bloom. We know that inspiration lies ultimately and abundantly within the genius of Mother Nature herself. She and we are interconnected; plugging back into nature is re-connecting with ourselves and there is a direct line to authenticity right there.

Wherever you find what makes you buzz – in a meadow, in your larder or in the Met – carry this pure and high vibration back with you and into your art when it taps you on the shoulder, and beckons you to your creative hub once more.

Why Now, Why Me?

There are many reasons why we might hit a block of some kind. Sometimes it will be an understandable falter after a knock. Has there been a specific event/non-event/wipe out/point of rejection that has set it off? It can be easier to get back up again when we know what shoved us over. Sometimes we try to force it too hard. Sometimes it will be shrapnel from a growth spurt. Sometimes it will come amidst coping with the general vagaries of life. Sometimes it will feel totally inexplicable. Sometimes it will be due to that creeping gripping worry of not measuring up to expectations – our own or others' – of just 'not being good enough' (more on this meddling minx to come). But it might help to know that you're in good company.

Join the Club

And it's quite a club. Just when, logically, you should have every technique in your psyche to successfully ward the beastly block off it can still catch up unawares. Most Creatives worth their supreme salt will hit barren land from time to time. Adele hit it after getting back to the studio following her (possibly intimidatingly) brilliant first album '19'. Sergei Rachmaninoff hit it dreadfully after his great friend and mentor Pyotr Tchaikovsky died. Peanuts cartoonist Charles Schulz suffered from writers block; his anthropomorphic beagle buddy Snoopy suffered from it too. Leo Tolstoy fell into the darkness for months at a time in between works of his literary genius. And the magnificent Claude Monet didn't escape it either. But he did go on after one of his longer difficult spells to paint one of his most beautiful (and ambitious) pieces ever. The rose-covered trellises at the entrance to his water garden at his home in Giverny in northern France comprise the 22 panels of the Grandes Decorations, installed at the Musée de l'Orangerie. Now that's what you call a comeback.

Conclusion: As long as we strive to push ourselves – and push ourselves we should – we will all come up against it at some point along this challenging path. So what are you going to do, seriously – not show up? Not continue? Not create? Not a chance.

Overall, friends, give yourselves a little time to shed that skin if you need to and park the guilt for taking the time to do so (I admit to struggling with this – cue shadow voices '*it's not going to paint itself you know*'). Choose to see it as a growth spurt. We are changing progressively and our approach to our art changes too. When the time is right and you're ready to resume again you'll know. (That or your editor/agent/client is knocking at the door! Don't panic – it's good to be needed!) Breathe out, up tools, and get your warrior whiskers back in the game.

To Précis –

When it's all going to pot remember: you and your art are not in combat. Ceasefire. Make peace. Build a bridge. Your creativity is your friend and you are on the same side. Work together.

If the basics aren't syncing and you're wading through treacle, step back and shift gears.

Get outside of yourself and get inspired. Even a day or two can make all the difference. Do it.

Remind yourself what drew you to your art – back to grass roots.

Look to your heroes and all that creative brilliance that has gone before.

Just look – anywhere but inwards.

DO pick up Julia Cameron's '*The Artist's Way*' for a full-on methodology spread out over 12 weeks to combat critical blocks. It is superbly effective.

Turn your block into a building block – or even a plinth! Use it. It's about transition, evolution, progression and growth.

Creative blocks are perplexing of course, but we can usually find a way to cope with them and to break them down. Black clouds gathering and descending however, are a very different story – we can soon begin to feel as if we have lost all sense of solid ground. If depression doesn't affect you – feel free to leapfrog to Section IV. For those it does, the next chapter I hope will help you to shore up your foundations to withstand all storms. Enter the only dog I've ever disliked...

Chapter 8

LE CHIEN NOIR

'There is a crack in everything, that's how the light gets in'

— Leonard Cohen —

Singer, Songwriter, Poet and Novelist

I am addressing here the debilitating matter of depression. This fellow is a game-changer. How to be brilliant when you can't even get out of bed? Caught in a loop of overthinking and negative thinking and gaining momentum on a downward spiral – everything feels so complicated, difficult, impossible. Depression is a very real and very challenging state of affairs when it descends.

I'm not suggesting it is part and parcel of the creative life – not at all. But it is also true that many in the arts are prone to giving this old boy shelter, in varying degrees.

Some will manage to create on through: it may not surprise you that Edvard Munch even saw his sufferings as part of himself and his art and believed that without them his art would be destroyed. Van Gogh of course painted prolifically through his pain, with impassioned brushwork, and brilliance, all his life. Some will find solace in their creativity, others will need to step back. Beethoven took seven years, from 1813, during which he wrote just one string quartet: aptly entitled 'Serioso'. Everyone to their own. What feels right for you, will be exactly right for you.

It is important for those of us who are so prone to have some tools to manage him so that if he should pay you a visit he doesn't decide to move in. I am not making light of this – and I'm not referring to an occasional down day. At my lowest point (and by 'point' I mean a huge plateau, as far as the eye could see) I could no longer see colour. I woke up one day and the world was an old black and white movie – in slow motion; voices muted and far away, colour gone, washed out, nothing. Not metaphorically but quite literally – actually perceptually – gone. So if you have your own black dog, I've been to the same wretched kennels, and know just how despairing it is.

I have however in the past been lucky enough to find various wonderful people, pathways and writings that helped me banish this unwelcome guest and get me through to the other side. And these days I'm all for a head-on eye to eye should I see his cast shadow looming down the line.

My Black Dog Toolkit: Having been through it on and off since my 20s, this is what I have learned:

1. **Don't identify with being depressed**: When you begin to understand that 'it' is not 'you', it's only passing through you, hope finds a way of creeping back in and somewhere on the horizon you catch that glimmer of blue. This nugget from Dr Tony Bates, clinical psychologist and writer on the subject, struck me deeply and in a way set me free. You 'are' not depressed. Realise (love this word – see with your 'real eyes') that this is not 'you' or who you are – you have a depression passing through you. This enabled me to detach from what I was going through, to see it as

a phase, and my mother's words to me each day that 'it will pass' began to ring true.

2. **Slow down**: Take some time, and vehemently swerve those who bring you down or whose problems only compound yours. Avoid those who Julia Cameron calls '*the crazy makers*' – let them go be crazy elsewhere. Get someone on the phone – but only someone who *gets* you – a close friend who will show you kindness and compassion. You needn't necessarily lean on them – talk about ANYTHING, just breaking the monologue opens the door ajar for a better conversation with yourself. The boys and men amongst you, please take note, I know the sisterhood is naturally more predisposed to 'the chat', and this vulnerability is *hard*, but jump the stereotype and get those words out – it really helps.

3. **Seek outside help**: I hated being an on-going drain on my loved ones, day in day out; it wasn't fair on them and I needed a healthy outside perspective. I needed to just get through it, and now I know I can – which is immeasurably liberating in itself. It took some external help to actually get a handle on it.

   I think many, especially in borderline depression, are loathe to seek therapy because they think then, by definition 'they're broken'. Well, if I was, I was excellently put back together. And to be honest, who in their right minds would head out into this precarious world feeling a little vulnerable without full combat gear? If you're human (*check*) and you need it (*sometimes, check*), and you can afford it (*I know, ouch, see below*) go get it.

   The *only* downside to external help can be the cost. But sometimes you have to cough up – especially if you, your art, and your loved ones are suffering because of this crushing condition. And having done it once, you may well learn the tools to manage it in future – so think of it as an investment. Write up notes immediately after your sessions so you have techniques and sensible perspectives to revert back to in the short and the long run. I still refer to mine ten years later when I need to.

If private therapy isn't an option, talk to your regular GP. Find out what services are available in your area and ask for a referral. Even being on a waiting list is a comfort in some way. Alternatively, get online and find the right phone number to ring. Mind (www.mind.org.uk) are a brilliant first port of call, www.supportline.org.uk will also give you various numbers for support systems that can help. Also www.itsgoodtotalk.org.uk has an easy to bite 'how to get therapy' (non-paying options included) section on its website too. In Ireland www.aware.ie is a super support platform, as is www.mentalhealthireland.ie which also details other organisations that you can contact (as relevant), and how. The Samaritans www.samaritans.org are always there and ready to help you too.

And don't entirely dismiss the (often automatic) suggestion of some medication. Many are anti-medication on point of principle, but if my body needs the fine-tuning I don't stand in its way. An SSRI can, for many, be an excellent way to start the day.

4. **What's the point?**: At a particularly low time I had an inner voice loud and clear on circular repeat … 'What's the point? What's the point in anything? What's the point of even getting out of bed let alone ANYTHING ELSE?' Well – ok. That day you may well feel, quite, there is no point. But what if, maybe, there might, elusively, surreptitiously, inconveniently, actually, be a point? Even a teeny one? In which case … if there *might* be a point, what's the harm in trying to see if there actually is and if so what it might be? There may well be none and if so back to the duvet with you with

an I-told-you-so, but you will have tried which is all any human level of existence can ask of itself when experiencing that emptiness we can feel. And I think you might find yourself feeling incrementally more human for having gone there. That cup in the sink needs washing. Even this feels big on the bad days. But you get yourself to wash it. Having done that – you might just take the next step and dry it. Before you know it, it is inviting you to make a fresh mint tea. You go to the mint plant on the windowsill – enter the power of Mother Nature and a restorative few minutes that taste warm and good. I promise you – it's the little steps. If you can take even one positive step to counter the negativity pervading, hurray for you.

And here's the thing – even with the most tentative of endeavours you may just have started making something beautiful in the process. (Besides a comforting cup). Get through it. Use it if you can at all. Even if you don't feel like it, try it. For me. (And for you and for those who love you. And for your art.)

5. **Chiaroscuro – as in art, in life**: Chiaroscuro is a foundational technique in approaching painting, darkest darks vs. lightest lights. I have learned in life too that only by experiencing the darkest darks can we know the lightest lights. It's the counterpoint – the juxtapose against the black night sky that will make the star shine brightest. Having been through the darkness and out the other side you can be assured my blessings have been well and truly counted. Depression can be hugely debilitating but it also presents us with an opportunity to appreciate, to dig deep and to grow. We develop depths of resourcefulness and self-knowing that otherwise would remain unchanneled. Only now, years later, do I know this to be true. And if you can keep this foreign concept hovering ahead on the horizon, that some

teeny bit of good may transpire, it might somehow diminish, again even incrementally, the sense of futility we feel.

6. **Get into the long game**: Try to build a sense of wellbeing that no one can take away from you, to protect yourself and protect your work. Working on long-term wellbeing is the best way to insulate yourself from downswings in your mood. Depression is more than this, I know, but pre-empting those black clouds looming can only help the bigger picture. (A small suggestion for your wellbeing bank: doing something nice for someone else when you're feeling below par can help it lift – and anything that breaks our self-absorbing focus can be a welcome relief.)

7. **Get into the green game**: Turn your blues to greens. Spending time in nature is key to good mental health so get yourself to green spaces. Chemicals released by plants that we then inhale improve our mood and wellbeing. 'Shinrin Yoko' or 'forest bathing' (mindful exploration in a forest) is the new Japanese kid on the cortisol-lowering block. In a less extreme than 'I-need-to-find-a-forest' way, might a grassy park or a local woodland be tempting? Staying in your own back garden, there is unlimited satisfaction in nurturing a plant into being (and then managing to keep it alive). Mother some sleeping beauties coming into springtime. I may feel like curling up in the earth myself but this brave little bulb is shooting skywards to grow – such courage! Such optimism! There is heroic mini inspiration right in there.

8. **Get 'appy**: Headspace, Calm, Insight Timer or Buddhify are just a start – there are apps tailored to all ages and states of mind. Or forearm yourself with something from the pool of podcast help. Listening to others' experiences in life, when they have felt

less than fabulous or even adequate, can help through a sense of trenches comradery, sharing advice or even raising a smile. Elizabeth Day's 'How to Fail' podcast is a favourite of millions (and mine). Her reassuringly honest discussions '*celebrating things that haven't gone right*' (her words), help us listeners to feel someway reconnected to the familiarly flawed self, to others and to life. In the bleaker moments perhaps just consider tuning in somehow to the world beyond your bunker. You'd be amazed at the messages and life-gems that sow their welcome seeds when we do.

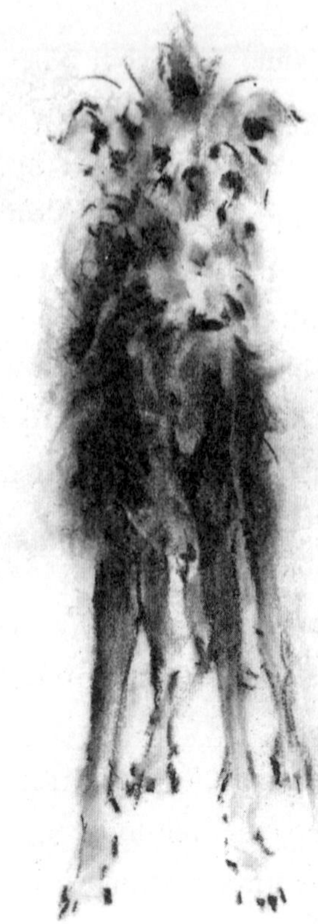

The Bottom Line: In the challenging times, try to show up in your life in whatever way you can. Do your best with the tools you've got on a given day. You might be sailing stormy seas at quarter mast but hold on tight until the sun shines for you once more. It will. Treat yourself with kindness – give yourself credit. And a big fat break. Don't sweat the small stuff as it comes and goes. Invest your energy in something more worthwhile (you). Understand that life is made up of many multi-faceted chapters and this is absolutely not going to be the one to unhinge you.

Not one bit.

PS: The Power of a Smile. I am including a little poem by F. Scott Fitzgerald here that touched me. It was one of my formulas for getting through the bad days:

'It was only a sunny smile,
and little it cost in the giving,
but like morning light it scattered the night
and made the day worth living'.

The domino effect of a smile is an amazing thing, and if you can put it out there it will shine back to you. Try to muster it. It's those little things that sometimes make just the difference in your day that you need.

SECTION IV: RECOVER

These are quite some travels we have embarked on – whoever said art was relaxing?!

When your art and your heart have been through trauma, it can be hard to remember where you left your mojo, or what it ever even looked like. Your enthusiasm, energy and confidence have taken a hit and the Creative you feels like a distant spectre. *Was that me? Was that even this lifetime? Was I really ever that brave?* Yes, yes and definitely yes and soon you'll be poised again and ready for more.

The following chapters will help dust down your finest moves and unveil pirouettes you didn't even know you could do. **Chapter 9** will help you to reconnect to your creative self and restart your studio processes. **Chapter 10** will optimise this comeback in the context of correct curating – looking to the benefits, and the beauty of space. **Chapter 11** includes some life hacks for when life hits you in the head. And it does, but you've got this. Shimmy on.

Chapter 9

RE-MOTIVATION

'One life. Just one. Why aren't we running like we are on fire towards our wildest dreams?'

— Anon —

Right team. About that higher ground.

Finding your motivation again is the first step in recovery when, for whatever reason, we have felt like creative roadkill. It can be hard when you're working on your own to reignite that flame of enthusiasm, so make it a feel-good welcome back. Having strategies to hand to speed up the recovery time is essential – think of yourself as an artistic athlete, and the following as isotonic assistance:

1. **Set your comeback scene**: Time to alter the attitude, the thinking patterns and the tune. Light a candle (the ones you save for guests), pour your cuppa in a cup without a chip, throw in a biscuit. Play Mozart's Symphony No.5 or hang a disco ball

or whatever floats your boat. On Monday mornings, way back when, on my commute to my city office (which always felt like recovery mode) I would buy pink tulips to get me through the week. A bit too *Legally Blonde* I know – it was never really going to work.

2. **Clear the decks**: You can't give a great performance from a place of chaos. Take a fresh look at your creative space. I found it really made a difference in my latest meltdown recovery to eject a few pieces that made me wince/blush/swear. I felt they were pulling me backwards to the less proud moments in my past when instead I needed to feel hopeful and future facing. It also helped putting away the almost-finished pieces I couldn't quite get right, completely out of sight, perhaps to return to when my attitude had shifted, or perhaps not. Sometimes what was you yesterday just isn't you anymore.

3. **Clear the mind decks**: Simplify where you are going. Then with one foot in front of the other take those first few baby steps. Set small goals in early days – and then think bigger as to what you want to achieve this week, then this month. Think sankalpa, plus schedule. A sense of purpose and accomplishment can be our carrot and our cake. You might be slow to begin with and all takes longer than you expected – that's no problem. We all know getting going really is the hard part.

4. **Step aside**: Should the self-limiting sabotaging begin to raise its voice, get out of your own way. To do this you may have to get out of your own head. Use your tools from Chapter 6: the brain has the wherewithal for resetting itself and getting back into balance if the mechanics are given a chance. You need to engage in the

present with your current potential. You don't need to find the 'old magic' – it is the new magic we are interested in now.

5. **Step outside**: You might want to move decks to feel re-invigorated? Take your instrument out of your practice room or your laptop to a café. A fresh change of scene and alternative ambience might be just what you need.

6. **Reach out**: To find that right vibration it might help to have a conversation with someone who is on your wavelength; a creative ally (preferably an optimist) who shares your common ground. Sharing of energy and ideas is a healthy kick-start and it can breathe new life into our thinking. Just as in a tennis knock-up, we're so often better when we're making shapes with someone who raises our game.

   This can be as little as a coffee, and as much as a collaboration. In fact the collaborative process in some artistic disciplines can spark pure magic. If you feel like your creative batteries are low, the time might be right for a co-write or co-production. Most of the great singer songwriters see teamwork as greater than the sum of its individual parts – and aren't we so glad they do?! Thank you Bowie & Jagger, George & Aretha (did I mention it's also really fun?) and all the other dynamic duos we've had the pleasure of thus far. Bryan Adams' co-write with Mutt Lange in 1991 still holds the 16-week record for a hit single at number one, all these years later. He said of the process *'Writing "Everything I Do" with Mutt took about 45 minutes and it was a moment that I've only felt a few times – it's the moment when you know it's a good song – it wrote itself.'* Ahh… The yummy soul stuff. Amazing things happen with amazing minds together.

7. **Shift your focus**: Take the pressure off yourself from completing a particular project/commission/script. I know this is hard under a looming sense of urgency but just see if you can recapture the delight that had you carve out that studio space in the first place. Give yourself an open opportunity to create something from nothing – expecting nothing back. Buddhists say that peace comes when expectations end. Get playful! Let those anxieties slide out and joyful engagement slip back in.

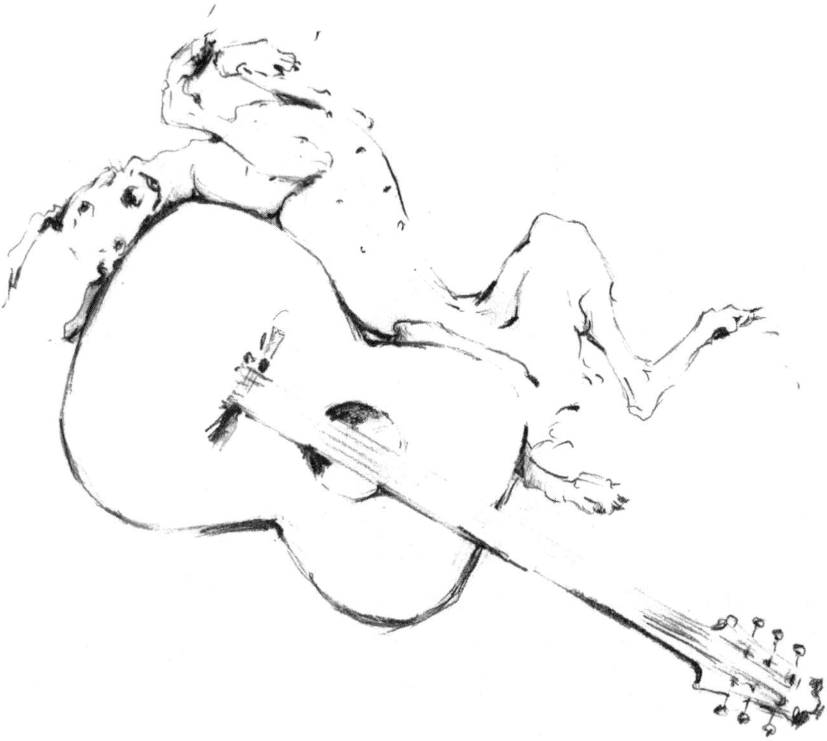

8. **Freestyle**: Try for a short time to chuck out your routine and rule book and sink into the embrace of the feel-good state of freedom that freestyling brings. Consider yourself a restriction free zone.

Don't overthink – improvise. Go bite-sized to begin – if you even do a doodle a day in 30 days' time you won't have a block and you might have an exhibition. Writers – think in terms of short spurts too – blog sized not book sized – but write them only for you to really go for it. You might surprise yourself with a project ready to launch in the process, but don't set out with this intention or you'll cramp your flow.

9. **Don't panic**: There's bound to be a little inertia when you're in recovery (or indeed, at *any* time – but particularly mid-recovery). Don't sweat it. Clearly no-one can bring their A-game every time and some days we just aren't flourishing. I could mount a strong argument for going back to bed or catching a matinee on days like these but better to say to yourself: *Do just one thing.* One thing, as we know, often leads to another one thing, and before you know it you may be writing a symphony. Or not. The point is that you're in it for the long ride and the less progressive days are inevitable and natural and human and necessary. Rock up anyway – a masterpiece or a learning curve – it will be what it's meant to be.

10. **Ditch the 'bigness' of it all**: Accept that you won't, can't, be an amazing creator all the time. We know that's not how it works. Accept that this has been a break and a time for new growth. Don't catastrophise before you even begin. Opt for 'I can' over 'I can't' at every turn ahead. Believe in your overall vision and accept that to get there is just an accumulation of manageable moves. Then be prepared to pedal hard and KNOW you're on your way.

11. **Up the skillset**: Whether tuition videos from your hammock or some real-life tuition, different teachers have very different lessons to teach you. Or even just to remind you what you forgot

you already know. I rarely come away without gleaning at least one helpful something and that one something can be just the bridge to recovery you need. More on this in Chapter 14.

12. **Up the resolution!**: That there will be no more endless dark nights of the soul. If it's threatening, paint or write or dance or play your air guitar with abandon. In your pyjamas. For three days solid. You are enough. If a little deranged. Get your act together, no time like now – you're ready.

And for all things re-motivating, uplifting and totally inspiring go to Elizabeth Gilbert's glorious *Big Magic*. It's slam dunk five-star wonderful and should be compulsory reading for anyone on this crazy path. She writes of how this world is inhabited not only by animals, plants, bacteria and viruses but also by ideas – '*a disembodied energetic life form*' that needs to manifest itself in collaboration with a human creative partner '*to be escorted out of the ether into the realm of the actual.*' She describes these ideas as swirling around searching for the right somebody, trying to catch their attention, to wave them down, organising coincidences and portents to pique their interest until they decide whether this one is for them. Should they transpire not to be: '*I always try to use my most gracious manners when sending an idea away; you don't want word getting around the universe that you're difficult to work with.*' Fabulous, groovy and brilliant – we need ALL the help we can get.

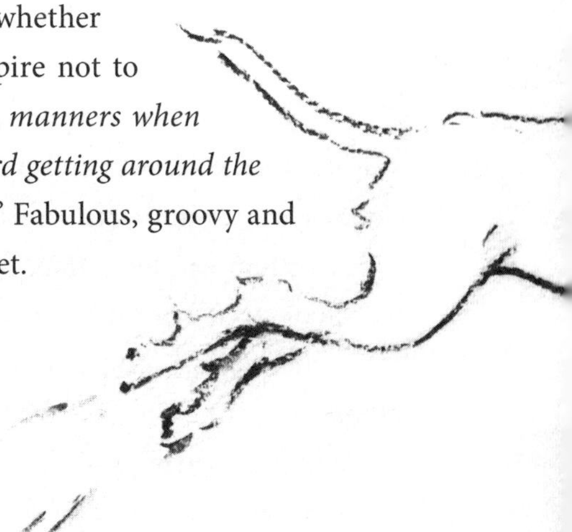

What are you doing still reading this? Go read her. (SERIOUSLY – Still here? Go!)

Chapter 10

SPACE, MAN

'For a seed to achieve its greatest expression, it must come completely undone. The shell cracks, its insides come out and everything changes. To someone who doesn't understand growth, it would look like complete destruction.'

— Cynthia Occelli —

Author, Entrepreneur, Dreamfollower

One word – regeneration. Regeneration requires optimising conditions. Recovery to full-on brilliant you will involve giving yourself a bit of space around your work.

Transitions can take time. You may have to set any ideas about speed and quantity to one side, even when your commission deadline calls (sorry client/agent/producer). Having said that if you are at the point of relying on your creativity for your income don't go burying your telephone and alienating the clients you worked so hard to get. (Also legal alert – be aware of contract stipulations – communicate, communicate.) If you need to take some unplanned time out most people understand that we can't always produce on demand. This is part of the frustration (and charm?) that is being a Creative.

Consider the following:

The Time Out Space

The Inner Space

The Compositional Space.

The 'Time Out' Space: Many will want to push on through a block or an episode of depression, and I totally understand if you do. The more serious we are about our creativity the more we want to just get on with it. Generally, I will take minimum time away from my tools as the feeling of futility at not producing doubles down heavily on the heaviness already there. For those of us relying on our art for our income there is an added and very real stress in that. Also, the longer away sometimes the harder it is to return – back in the saddle and all of that.

The thing is, however, whether working through a block or blip or even whistling along on an even keel, time out is time well spent. It may ultimately prove more efficient. Sometimes we will benefit from stepping back to regain clarity on our bigger picture. We need to take time to absorb new changes and to open ourselves up to new inspirations as they make their way in.

If the guilt is eating in, or you feel you need a permission slip, take this on board: '*When you're not painting, you're painting*'. Starting out, I didn't understand when my clever tutor (and brilliant portrait artist), Nick Bashall, said this to me. I thought he was just compulsively obsessed. In fact, he recognised early on the vital importance of creating space in our creativity too. It has taken me quite a time to work out that some of the important breakthroughs come when we take a step back. Not only when we are wrung out or burnt out but also when firing on all cylinders too. Time away is still time invested. Our tools may be at rest but a Creative's subconscious (for better for worse!) is always at work.

Taking space will keep our instincts fresh. To work incessantly can mean our creative thinking skills becoming dulled and routined and blurred. We are less likely to default to autopilot when we see thing anew and this is important to keep producing at our best. Plus we get opportunities to fill the well. Charles Dickens, for example, as part of his writing routine, used to walk a dozen miles through the city of London at night. He believed that this time spent living and breathing the world of his subjects was just as vital to his craft as the five hours a day spent at his desk. He would go out to bring his world in and for him it brought his work and his characters alive.

Of course there are times of production pressure when you've really got to go for it, and you will know when this is necessary, and important. But sometimes we get stuck when we get too stuck in. There are precious benefits – beyond mere relaxation and enjoyment – which lie in reading the Sunday papers or chatting with friends. It is in these times that a really good idea will just waft across the front of your brain – the one you had been manically chasing/trying to pin down – and all you need to do is reach out and take it. Glory be.

The Inner Space: Back to creating space between your thoughts. A relaxed and clutter-free mind will allow that clear landing space for the creative forces to come back into play. I won't bang on anymore about it but with your own 'noise' on silent mode, you might just get back to the gap to pick up some invaluable creative clues. Or at the very least, don't knock it, you might find some inner peace. You're welcome.

The Compositional Space: Using space *within* our work, compositionally, has the capacity to propel the good to great. This concept is relevant of course at all stages of creativity, not just post-recovery. I have included it at this point, however, as it is a style that tends to develop as we develop as Creatives. As we grow we have the confidence not to fill in the silences. Too much noise can prove a riot on the senses – we need resting spaces in the rhythms too. Whether writing a novel or painting a portrait – it is finding the quiet notes in pace/tone/canvas corners that provide the backbone for the substance of what we really want to convey.

Take music. The magic of experiencing music is often said to lie in the no-notes between the notes. As Miles Davis said '*It's not the notes you play but the notes you don't play*'; it's not the notes that impact but the juxtaposition with the quiet spaces between them. Thereafter varying the timing of a no-note can have an arresting effect, injecting pathos and structure and strength. And of course, the gentler sotto voce expressions are often the ones that strum the soul strings. Be intuitive as to when we might need to rest in them awhile.

And writing. Writers of fiction will know the importance of pacing in storytelling and mastering the ebb and flow throughout. Even the highest paced plotlines are strengthened by including resting places too. As readers we need to absorb and digest before we take flight again: bring us with you while keeping us hooked in for more. The gentle spaces are the mesh, the glue, the armature, that make the delivery work as a whole.

For thespians, the strength in the dramatic pause speaks, or doesn't, for itself. Creating tension, releasing tension, allowing for processing – all vital to the delivery too.

In my own discipline, I love the confidence to omit what is 'unnecessary' when superfluous to the purpose of a work. There is strength in the power of suggestion, the confidence of omission and a little smokiness – typically these are the paintings and sculptures that speak to me. There is joy in the unspecified: the buttery waves of a Troubetzkoy bronze capturing a light-hearted confident energy of a jolly studio sitting. For me this is genius. Not just deliciously aesthetically pleasing: it transports me to the St Petersburg studio with model muse and probably her dogs (along with all his other studio animals – bear, fox, wolf – it was all happening) in a belle epoque gone by. Space can take the audience through time and ... well, space.

The beauty of compositional negative spaces lies in their power to engage the beholder/listener/reader as a participant in the creative work and not just an onlooker or passer-by. There is an invitation to participate, to finish what was started, by what is left unsaid in blurring edges, the place where 'no thing' ends and another thing begins – or doesn't. Contrasted with explicit expression towards which the focus is pulled, cleverly pulling us in towards what pulled the artist in too. I love the playfulness, infused into the skilfulness, allowed for by confidence! This is the energy that abounds, and we, beyond the edges of the creative work, feel it too.

As a Creative, don't feel you always need to close your questions with answers – that line untold, that detail unspoken, that edge unfound – there is joy in the liminal fringes. The 'unsaid' allows for the artist's truth to connect to something true within individuals of the audience too. It can be a bridge to allow for interpretation of what the beholder perceives it, or needs it, to be. Allow for the quiet spaces, man – they are strong, and they are golden.

#Space...Man

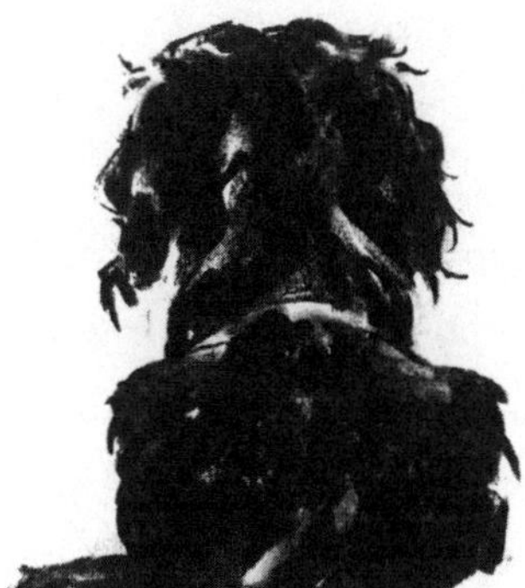

Chapter 11

I SPY A BLUE SKY

'Nothing is impossible. The word itself says "I'm possible".'

— Audrey Hepburn —

Actress and Humanitarian

So, your wings are spread and you are taking flight. Phew and wonderful. If this was a Disney movie, your journey of self-discovery would now be behind you, and you would be embarking on a smooth path to fulfilment, recognition and rewards. (Also, probably, a royal spouse somewhere along the way.) But the creative life – all life – is a journey (and we tend to keep kissing frogs!). There will be no closing credits (until *the* closing credits). You've come a heck of a distance to soar above the clouds but we're still short on the fairy tale.

Things won't always go smoothly. In art or in life. The trick is to get solution orientated. Take faith from knowing that even stabbing a painting right through doesn't always spell The End. (It was a bad day for an artist friend, and a busy one for a wonderful art restorer). Sharpen those survival instincts and have help on standby – remember you are in this for the long game.

To keep mental disruption at a minimum moving forward and to keep on keeping on, this is what I want you to do:

- **Remain inquisitive**: Develop the habit of questioning and seeking to push yourself to higher ground. Read inspiring material and follow Creatives whose work touches your soul – it would help to get savvy on social media for this (more later). Look around (and up!) and always be open to learning. Don't stalk but do investigate. Keep tapping that inspiration going forward. When nothing creative is coming out, you might need to put some creative in.
- **Remain self-centred**: In a good way. Fulfilment comes from us meeting our own expectations, not the expectations of others. Hitching our sense of self-worth to whims and forces beyond ourselves leads, at best, to transient moments of contentment and has the power to derail us completely.
- **Remain resilient**: Believe in your endeavours. As a Creative we have to hang ourselves out there on the great dart board of life. I, for one, am tremendously easily upset, and often thrown by a wrong intonation in feedback or nuance that makes me want to shout: 'You just don't get me'. Please try not to be floored by the criticisms of others – more on this to come. Stay high.
- **Remain balanced**: Develop a habit of looking at what is going right. Remember your winningest and proudest moments so far and draw on them when the self-doubt starts to creep in.
- **Remain intact**: Keep your counsel until 'showtime' with, at the most, a trusted few whose opinions you value and advice you treasure. Those who know you, know your essence and know your work. This way you can remain on your truest path

unfettered by the ebb and flow of external favour (you ain't going to please them all).

- **Remain focused**: Retain that higher vision – your vision is what matters. Don't be deterred or intimidated by factors beyond your control. When you stop worrying about what has or hasn't occured for you creatively in the past – and quit worrying that things in the future might not go as planned, it sets you free. Then you will be in the present moment, and we know that's where it's all to play for.

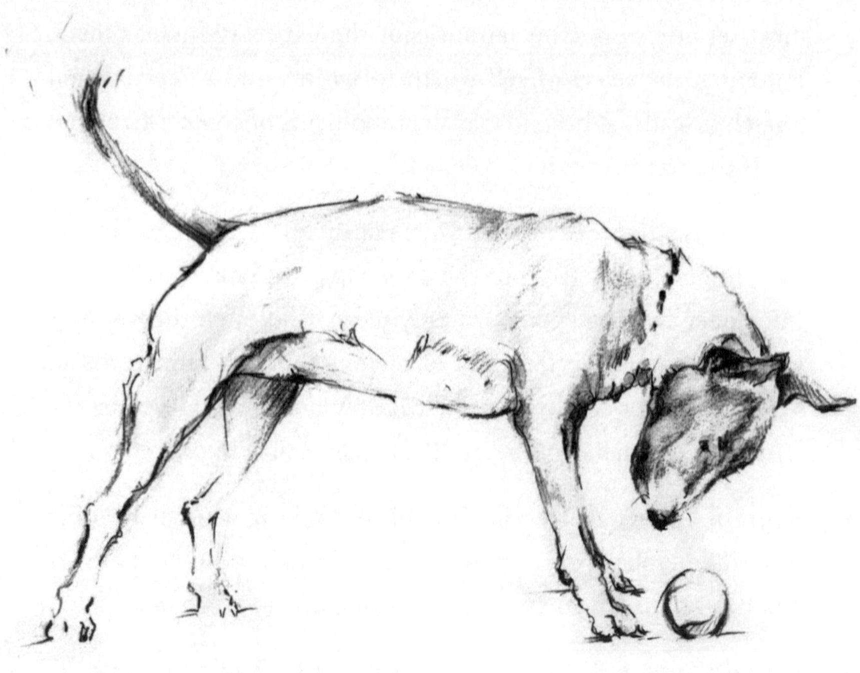

- **Just remain**: Sometimes I think we deserve a pat on the back for simply showing up. Consider yourself applauded.

- **Patience, sweet patience**: I find this hard, I'm more a time-is-of-the-essence girl. But sometimes a little patience is necessary for the perfect storm to come together to create something dynamic and important. I've had paintings I really believed in that returned home, tail between their legs, from their debut forays out into the world. I mourned their (my) failure, only to find I needed them for something bigger and better down the line. It turned out that they were biding their time (I just wasn't party to their schedules as yet). I've also had work that I considered complete but, having the benefit of spending some extra downtime together, I realised needed a little extra chutzpah – the angostura bitters to the champagne cocktail (who knew it could get *even* better!). Many writers will find the same. Sometimes we wait for our art, sometimes its waits for us. When the moment is right it will happen. Timing in life is all.

On your upward soar, you're going to hit turbulence – often. You may have yours already, but these are my recommended life shimmies:

Have on speed dial:

Your cheerleaders (friends, dear friends)

A handyman who is exactly that

A wing woman (she may be called Thelma, in which case know where the handbrake is)

A good therapist for when life starts getting in our faces

A good facialist, for when we start wearing life on our faces

Someone to laugh with when we do

A platonic member of the opposite sex who brings wit, wisdom and wine on demand

A good restorer for any hapless stabbings (see above …)

Need to learn:

Car lore

Fusebox stuff

How your phone works

To take compliments

To lose gracefully

To succeed gracefully

To own it when you make a mistake

To forgive others

To forgive ourselves

To make vodka jelly

To back up your hard drive

Basic DIY.

Need to remember:

To breathe

To listen more

To exit the house looking clean, and sane, every day

To switch focus from what's going wrong to what's going right

SPF50 every day

To relax

To allow ourselves to be happy.

SECTION V: KICK OFF THE COVERS

Blocks and beasties behind us, these are infinitely better days – the potential is palpable! We all know that evolving as an artist will still conjure up some testing moments as we take our work out into world. It's just part of the process, entirely to be expected, and you might check for a pulse if it didn't. This is life in all its complex glory and, irritatingly, there are always going to be factors that will come in to kill our creative buzz. You need firstly to address them, possibly embrace them, and then go on to manage them. All of this you can do.

Fear, criticism and their first cousins are just part of a Creative's laundry pile – things to be dealt with, but not to get you down. **Chapters 12** and **13** will help you in ironing them out. Confidence will oscillate. There may even be times when you feel like a fraud or a fake. **Chapter 14** looks to shooing these naughty shadow voices away. Remember – the keys to our creative expansion lie in how we face up to the many moments that try us – less 'apologetic', more 'world beating' please. **Chapter 15** is your final cross check before take-off – courage mes braves.

Through any incidental commotion, keep your focus on the bigger deal here – you are a Creative who gets to create – the rest we can totally handle.

Chapter 12

HELLO FEAR

'Fear is the raw material from which courage is manufactured. Without it we wouldn't even know what it means to be brave.'

— Martha Beck —

Author and Life Coach

Fear of failure tends to be the greatest reason for either not performing as we might (the old stage fright chestnut) or generally not starting. Can't start, can't fail, won't fail – winning at life! Sorry, but no.

Thereafter, fear around the 'acceptability' of our work, of not being enough, the trickling away of confidence and trickling in of procrastination – are these ringing any bells? Overwhelm then moves in where we find ourselves behind in our progress, beyond our comfort zones and generally out of control. The more overwhelmed we feel, the more likely we are to disconnect from rational, constructive thinking and either back away, or 'up the struggle' until finally, we sink.

THE GOOD NEWS! I have come to learn that once our underlying feelings towards our work, our audiences, and ourselves are looked at properly, and addressed sensitively and sensibly, then fear and overwhelm may be managed, and managed pretty well.

Here's what I'm thinking:

Rethinking Our Thinking

Developing New Thinking

Not Thinking.

Rethinking Our Thinking

If we are serious about our creativity then just 'thinking positively' really doesn't get us far; thinking real and *processing positively* does:

- **Challenge your choices**: We have a choice not to fear. If we can stop and look at how we are thinking about something, we can address and actually decide how we are going to feel about this something. We take back ownership of our thinking (and hence of our fears) to give us the best chance going forward.

  To do this you need to get out of your head and into the role of your own best friend. (It doesn't necessarily mean you open the wine and go find a dancefloor although I'm not ruling that out). This friend sees things clearly, objectively and how they really are. He will give it to you straight. Just because you didn't have a sell-out show does not mean you're a failure as an artist. Seven publishing house rejections *is* par for the course. One bad theatre review absolutely does not a bad actor (or writer, director or set designer) make.

  To disengage from the 'beat me up' default thinking before it takes its toll, take a moment to cross-examine it. Just because not *everybody* likes your paintings, does it automatically follow you are a terrible painter? Is that even logical? Might you be catastrophising – even a teency bit? Van Gogh sold one in a lifetime – to his brother – come on! Choose to think better.

- **Challenge your 'Everybody'**: Question the omni powerful 'Everybody', as in: '*What will EVERYBODY think?*' We tend to appoint a supercritical hypothetical 'Everybody' as the chief barometer, judge and jury of how 'good' or 'bad' 'we are'. Who put this Everybody in charge of our heads? Oh man, again, we did.

  Take a good look at yours. Disassemble the Everybody into individuals – it helps. Martha Beck's teachings in her inspirational book *'Finding Your Own North Star'* give a master performance in this. Those we get hung up about are not always the Everybody that (a) matter or (b) would be the best source of data-gathering for us and our creativity anyway. (Note here the importance of connecting to your correct audience. Walt Disney had the wrong audience when he got fired from a newspaper because the editor thought that he had no imagination. Imagine ...)

  From here-on in, replace the looming 'Everybody' with a group of people that works. People who you respect and have *your* interests at heart. Their feedback might still sting a tad but this is (good?) pain you can use.

Developing New Thinking

You owe it to your creativity to develop more responsible responses. A bit of rewiring might be called for:

- **Demands, demands**: Because the creative life is not hard enough as it is, we also place irrational demands on ourselves that we wouldn't dream of imposing on a loved one (or even on a not-so-loved one). Your antennae should pop up when your self-talk moves along the lines of '*I must/I ought to/I've got to/I should…*'. Stop, catch them, slap them and switch them to kinder more achievable and realistic versions of what you are requiring of your creative self: 'it would be good if…'; 'I would be happier if…'. Please, give yourself a break.

- **Better banter**: When your chats with self are proving massively unhelpful, get some better ones going. Some suggested pivots:
    - *This is going to end badly* – **to** – *This might go really well!* Don't avoid a challenge – EMBRACE IT.
    - *This is too difficult and I'll never manage it* – **to** – *I'm going to give it my best shot* – Worse than failing is not trying.
    - *I can't see any point* – **to** – *There might just be a point and I might even learn something* – Always be open to progress.
    - *What if I bomb?* – **to** – *People might think this rocks* – It might and it would be terrible never to know…
    - *People will be critical* – **to** – *I might get valuable feedback to speed up the feedback loop* – That's always a win, or at least a silver lining.
    - *I'll never be as good as Banksy* – **to** – *I'm not as good as Banksy but he's a super inspiring original thinking risk-taker of the zeitgeist and I can learn a shedload from him* (The art-genius bit, not necessarily the moonlight-graffiti bit) Also: *And shur look, I'm getting better all the time!* (flip it flip it flip it…)

You get the gist.

Take your negative default assumptions and turn them into positive possible outcomes. Your spectre of failure flips to '*What if I succeed?*' Yaaay for that.

- **Better outlook**: The most desirable frame of mind going into your opening night (or *Bake Off* audition, or open mic night) is to presume it will be a cracker. That's the energy and momentum I want you to bring to it. If, however, you are finding yourself stalling beneath a fear cloud – you could have a conversation with yourself that goes something like this (adapt as necessary):

  'I would love my preview exhibition evening to go well but in reality it might not. If it doesn't, it doesn't mean that I can't be a successful artist – I will have a good body of work to send to an art fair/to approach a gallery/to sell elsewhere or I might be happier taking on commissions or teaching others, rather than just working to shows. When I regroup (mind, body and soul!) after the show I could explore new techniques or media or different subject matter that I've had an inkling to try? If it doesn't meet my highest hopes, well, I might learn from where it fell down … My marketing, my pricing, my palette right now? If it doesn't go brilliantly, I won't feel great about it but in reality, I can cope with it. In the worst-case scenario I will get feedback and build better from there going forward.'

  Then, if you have had a creative experience which feels more like a character- than a career-builder (ouch), try asking: '*Were there SOME people who liked what I did?*' Well yes, the applause felt genuine and great on the night even though ticket sales are slow. Or – '*Some of my paintings sold to some of the people, this means that not everybody hated what I did … This means some people really liked what I did*'. See how that went?! Might you think

> '*Well, I didn't completely star, but I did my best and go me for trying*'? Might you see what didn't go quite to plan and take that to build to a better performance next time? Might you think ... *Positively?* Yes, I think you might.

Not Thinking

When the fear swirls, try to shift gears into your present moment awareness (yes – again – sorry). When we inhabit a more mindful space then many pesky conjured fears will disappear all by themselves. Those that then remain can be addressed constructively, dissipated individually or transmuted to opportunities to grow. Above all we mustn't let fear immobilise us, or make us curl up in a hedgehog ball.

And Breathe... In hedgehog-ball scenarios use your conscious breathing as your anchor, to bring you back to here, to now, to you. Just stop everything, pause, and follow the flow of your breath, in, and out. Recalibrate, reconnect, then unfurl yourself into your creativity again. Did you know that the medical definition of inspire is 'to draw in by breathing', (from the Latin *inspirare*)? Your breath is your life force, physically and creatively – engage consciously with it when you need to.

Conclusion: If you remember just one thing from this chapter let it be this: fear is ultimately disempowered when we trust that we can handle anything that comes our way. '*I can handle it!*' (Susan Jeffers – *Feel the Fear and Do It Anyway* – she's brilliant btw) is more than an affirmation; used in the right way this is headspace gold. 'I can handle it', as a Creative, and as a human, is the single best mindset we can adopt. Whatever the object of our fears, it holds no real threat to us when we trust that, come what may, we could cope with it. This might involve looking at any potential outcome that you feel would get the better of you, and in reality, when you break it down, you can see that it won't break you. Even though it might be uncomfortable, painful or frustrating, equally it might be extraordinary. And our creative output into the world is worthy of taking that risk.

(**A caveat**: we must be brave but not naive. If there are fears around finances and other practicalities the basis of these must be examined carefully. We'll deal with the nuts and bolts of Creatives in business in Section VI. Assessing risks and thinking sensibly in a way that your numbers add up is part of your self-care too.)

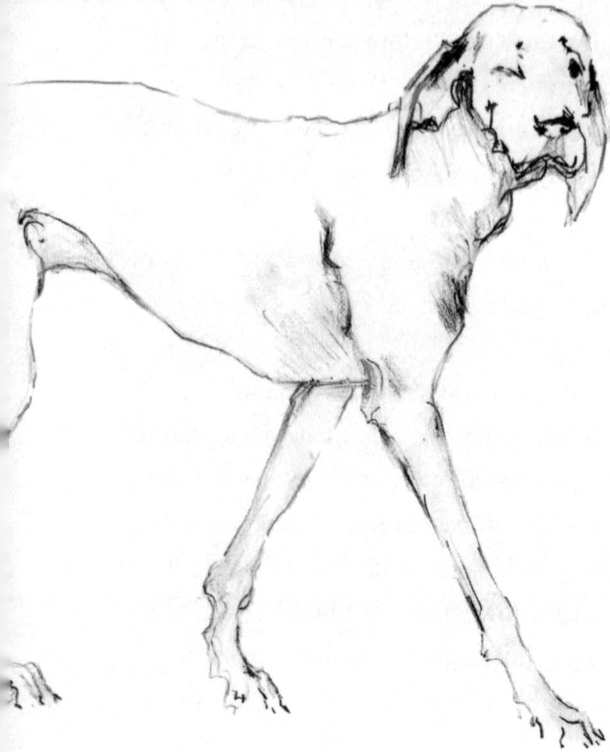

Some Thoughts About The F Word

Manage your mental housekeeping. If you can sustain an inner level of steadiness, your fears will feel smaller and your coping abilities stronger.

Fear can be dissolved in the context of self-appreciation. Look at where you started and how far you've come.

Think about times when things *have* worked out, plug into the joy and confidence this brings in and the fear will fizzle out.

Your fears might be useful – they might just motivate you to doubly prepare and be the best you can be. Use them as fuel.

Don't fake fearlessness – asking for help is right and sensible and strong.

Look at your 'Everybody' and know your 'Everybody' who matters. (Thank you Martha Beck.)

When you feel like hiding, you owe it to your creativity to face into your fear – an ostrich has never won an Oscar.

If it helps anyone – people, writing this book is terrifying – I am not 'a writer' but I think I have some knowledge that might be of benefit to others (or even just *an* other!) I am under no illusion that everyone will like it (cue next chapter) but I am putting it out there, despite the terror.

If I can, you can.

Chapter 13

HOWDY CRITICISM!

'Until you're ready to look foolish, you'll never have the possibility of being great.'

— Cher —

Singer, Actress, Creative Chameleon

Cher dares.

Conforming is always an option, if you want to be a closet Creative. Rather than conforming of course, you could throw in some innovative dynamite, shake things up a little, ruffle their feathers and generate some homespun effervescence.

Children of the '70s, do you remember 'space dust' – the popping sherbet candy that crackled in your mouth? These days champagne bubbles might hit the same happy note?! In any case that's what we are aiming for – inner sparkle.

To create sensationally in a sense that matters to you deep down, you have to be willing to carve your own groove, somehow. We can choose to follow steadily where others have furrowed – of course we can – but we will never high-five ourselves or fulfill our creative curiosity from there.

The truth is, you may need to be willing to run the risk of criticism if you're going to live true to yourself and give to your creativity the crackle and pop it needs.

Bring It On: As soon as you put your creativity out into the world you are starting a conversation. Inevitably we can't always predict how this goes. We know we can't control what other people think, but when they share their feedback we can totally control what we do with it. This is the key to staying in your power, and that's where we want you!

Four points about criticism:

1. People have a right to have their thoughts, even about our precious, heart-sourced work. We must be tolerant and demonstrate patience and resist the urge to 'take them down'.

2. We do have a right to believe they are wrong about our work, which they might well be. This is what the mute button is for.

3. Hey, they're talking about you! Is there anyone worthy of note that hasn't attracted criticism? Join the gallery of groundbreakers. Let's remember too that there exists a breed of people (especially online) who can only save themselves from drowning by pushing others under the water. Keep perspective. And a snorkel.

4. It is entirely up to us how we respond. Is their opinion useful for the feedback loop? Creative catalysts are always welcome. Or just plain irritating? Delete, delete, delete. The great thing is, it's up to you.

We generally need outside data to better our output. Taking criticism in the right way (the one that doesn't derail us) can be a fantastic opportunity to learn.

How Not to Let it Crush You: Respond in a way that is beneficial to you and your art. No knee-jerk reactions – in 'reacting' we fail to make conscious choices and quite frankly that is getting us nowhere. The simple tweak to start 'responding' instead of 'reacting' to all irritating circumstances will pay dividends in your bank account of life.

Your response might be proactive – to enquire more and understand fully the basis of the criticism, or it might be to do nothing at all. It might be to pivot and springboard from the learning, or to rejoice in your disruption of perceived ideals and carry on full throttle. It really doesn't matter, as long as you realise it's your call.

To Entertain or to Eject?: We constantly need to learn and grow but we also need to continue to create, undented. Where a critical viewpoint might just be valid, use it in a way that is constructive to you. Where it is unhelpful/destructive/says more about them than you, toss it away. You will learn to discern which is which. No matter how valid or helpful the criticism, I still smart a little to hear it – these are my babies they're talking about! But I put it into perspective and context, and if no good can come of it, I put it into the bin.

Some suggested responses as follows, (note that number 4 might be taken badly if said out loud):

1. *'I hear you, but I don't agree with you.'* Allow them their (erroneous!) judgement – you're not going to let them bring your happy day down.

2. *'You have a point!'* Can I learn from this? Great. This is GOOD criticism – always welcome. Happy to engage.

3. *'You might have a point...'* Does this person's opinion matter much when stacked against your own belief in your work? If so,

even if you don't agree with it, lean in to listen. If this person is someone whose input you value, take on board what they have to say. Listen, learn, fly higher. This is an opportunity, not a knock. Our path is constant evolution, and we are ever our own works in progress. Your more experienced self might regard this to have been a critical conversation to have had.

4. *'I'm not sure you have a point and I'm not sure about you.'* Do with this what you will – you might explore but wear it lightly and feel free to discard. (NB, reminder – sotto voce)

5. *'To be honest I'm perfectly happy with what I put out there.'* Ignore completely – see you later, adios, talk to the hand. Totally valid and sometimes the best!

Managing the Puncture Wound: Some tough love: *You* are the only one who can make yourself upset over what other people think or say. When a comment upsets you, you are upset by your feelings about that comment, and the meaning you are attaching to it. You are responsible not for others' words and actions, but for how you feel. Seriously, you're in charge. In the same way that you can choose not to fear, choosing not to feel upset is within your remit, difficult though that might be. But it is a conscious choice, and only you can make it. This is all well in theory – I hear you say – but is mighty hard when it's someone whose opinion matters to you. Of course I've been there too.

Some might say 'toughen up'. But as Creatives it is our sensitivity that keeps the channels open between our perceptions, our responses and our output. To close off a valve is not to do our flow any favours. My family would say that I am oversensitive generally, and I'd say they might be right. In knowing this, now, when feeling 'victimised' by valid criticism, I can (sometimes – I'm not going for honours here) park my instinct to sulk/be hurt and instead decide to soak up what might help me going forward. '*What's their problem with me?*' can flip to a eureka breakthrough if I listen up in a non-defensive headspace. I no longer want to slap them but kiss them! Perhaps I'm growing up.

Remember always, you can't build your sense of self on how others perceive you. This is to give them unwarranted power over your wellbeing and will end up driving you mad. We need to work towards a position of self-belief where we simply don't require another's approval. There are always going to be 'haters' – whatever we do in life! We can't put a gloss on them. Focus instead on the lovers, and keep perspective, always.

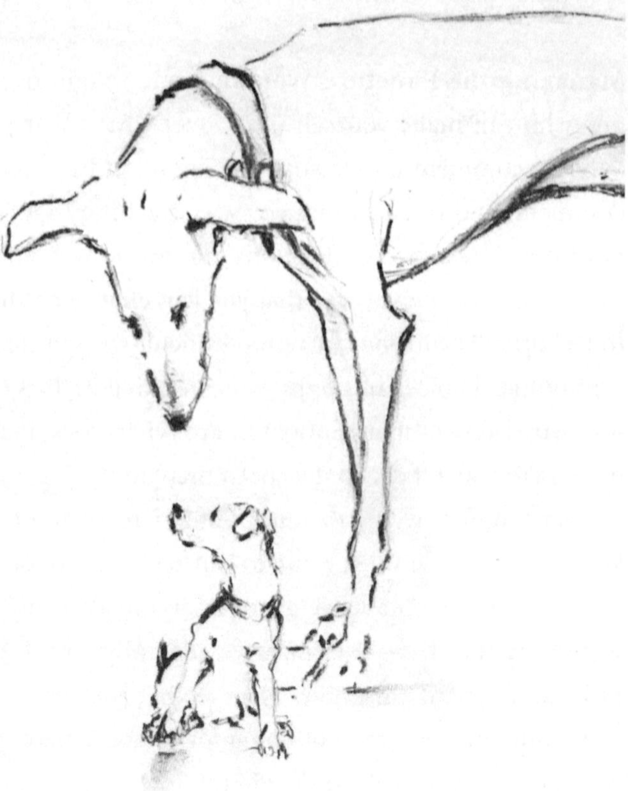

Chapter 14

IMPOSTER BEGONE ...

'If you hear a voice within you saying you cannot paint then by all means paint and that voice will be silenced.'

— Vincent Van Gogh —
Painter

When we step up to the stage, we sometimes hit episodes of low confidence when we believe ourselves to be less competent than others might perceive us to be. The gap between our perception and other's perceptions of 'how we are doing' allows the spectre of the imposter to step on through. Confusing? It really is – why on earth would we put such unnecessary obstacles in our own creative way?

The term 'imposter syndrome' grates on me but how it affects us grates on me even more. It steals our sunshine. Essentially, it encapsulates a fear of being judged in our performance of something that really matters to us, and to be found to be falling short. Even when we're ticking along just fine. Isn't that cruel? We lose faith in ourselves and our abilities and sometimes we are overwhelmed. Basically, we feel like we are faking it.

Sometimes there is a definite trigger. It might happen following an instance where things didn't go to our A-plan: the manuscript was rejected, a fluffed audition, the audience didn't show up or the red dots didn't flow. It might happen when life throws up unexpected challenges –a breakdown, a betrayal, even a pandemic. You are overwhelmed because it is overwhelming – there is a context to it. At other times it just creeps in regardless, for no reason beyond the mere fact of our being human.

For Creatives, imposter syndrome is more likely to come wrecking your head when you haven't had your time at Goldsmiths, RADA, NYU or the London School of Fashion and yet here you are with this brilliant raw unmoulded bundle of talent. In answer I share with you the not uncommon and compelling example of Andrew Scott as a panacea to your panic. Fleabag's-hot-priest-come-Sherlock's-evil-foe demonstrates (divinely and demonically) how far 'untrained' sheer talent can go. Whatever your calling, if you haven't been classically trained, please know that this just needn't be a disadvantage these days. Yes it's a wonderful opportunity – not least to meet others on your path – but it is CERTAINLY not the only way. There are always the great Universities of Life, of Practice and of Youtube, which are open to all.

If this is you, then you might consider a concentrated spell learning intensively with a great tutor. Whether it be night classes or a full-on week or month, this can be far more beneficial than years spent in the traditional system. Do your homework to find someone who you really want to learn from. It can be a way of gaining valuable training within focused parameters which work for you and your plan. If financial constraints are holding you back there are the options of apprenticeships and internships too. (If interning, make it work for you – a fixed period before review, and be sure to get good references from it too.) Perhaps you could even think to barter in some way – you might build their website or help in their office in return for their teaching wisdom. I paid for my Hamptons studio lodgings by painting a loveable labradoodle. We all have something of ourselves to offer.

If signing up for a workshop, a health and safety hard-hat warning: do expect at least one meltdown in the process. You often dismantle parts of what you know to build your game up again. You'd like to call it an awakening, but it is in fact a breakdown. Sometimes you've got to break things down to build them back up, and build them better.

There are some very worthwhile courses run regularly across the arts spectrum in this era of easy sharing – get googling. Right now you don't even have to leave your kitchen, thanks to the boom of Zoom. Ask your heroes if they do workshops – occasionally they do. (This obviously only applies to the living heroes. You won't get much response from the rest...) Why wouldn't you ask – for information, guidance or help? Don't ask, don't get, as the wise woman always says. If you don't ask – well then, you'll be landed with regret. And truly, regret is the most redundant of emotions. If you're afraid to ask, for fear of rejection, or because you don't feel worthy – well you've got to kick those emotions to the kerb I'm afraid. They're NFI'ed today.

Do all you can to build towards being the Creative you know you can be. The true antidote of feeling 'imposter-ish', however, lies not in an educational validation but in our own self-belief. The best way to build this up is to work hard and see your results increasingly shine. Once you connect into your authentic self and produce creative output true to this, the lurking ghouls won't get a look in. Especially – gloriously – when you find that audience who connects with it too.

Chapter 15

SELF-ACCEPTANCE

'This is me'

— You —
Work In Progress

The Creatives' default setting is self-critical at best. On a bad day we can really beat ourselves up. This isn't a satisfactory state of affairs and does zero good for our positive outlook. If I'm being honest however, it's often the case that Creatives who are always and consistently happy with their work tend to be either numb or deranged. Their progress is more of a flat trajectory, prone to ricocheting laterally between works, in a Groundhog Day sort of fashion. Self-criticism, if it has a positive, can be said to keep us developing and moving forward; being content with your output constantly would only lead to a loss of momentum to push personal and creative limits and explore new terrain, resulting in work which tends, dare I say it, to plateau.

The thing is, when we falter in our practices there is no one else to blame. Naturally we get stressed, but disproportionate stressing doesn't help the quality of your brushstrokes, or your iambic pentameters – plus it gives you wrinkles. Confidence building and being happy in our skin is a lifetime's work, but the more we practise the right attitude, the more natural it all becomes. Even when it's testing.

Coping with Failure: Deeply unpleasant perhaps, but failure is the foundation of our creative expansion. Fact. Layer upon layer if necessary, our failures are a rite of passage. Learning from them and surviving them make our work, and our resilience, stronger. The sooner we accept ourselves in all our failing glory the sooner our creativity will get up and out there. Then, only then, can we get on with being who we truly are.

So. Failures are tough, but necessary, and are, ironically, the foundation of our successes. Go with this:

- The most pioneering moments require tenacity and bravery, and the great achievements of our heroes are the culmination of many deaths on a studio floor which have gone before. Confidence may be knocked, but hang your hat on the knowledge that our failures precede our breakthroughs and ultimately inform our triumphs. And remember it's all practice; like an athlete or a sports pro, we have to go through the motions (and the psychological barriers) to work on our bigger game. It *will* eventually improve, so keep the winner's enclosure defiantly in your psyche throughout.

- Highly successful Creatives manage to flip their perception of 'failures' to fodder towards ultimate fruition. They don't let the 'under par' output dent their self-belief, incorporating it instead as an essential part of the process. The musical genius that is Ed Sheeran says that with songwriting you can never write a bad song that isn't worth it: '*Even if it's a bad song, you're getting it out of you. You've loads of good songs and bad songs in you so you've just got to make sure they come out bit by bit – you're unclogging the good songs in writing a bad one first*'. Fabulous, Mr. Sheeran.

I love the idea of an excited row of beautiful works lining up in an orderly fashion inside of me waiting for their turn to come out when the turkeys have upped and flown.

- My life: Paint. Fail. Learn. Grow. Paint Better. See?! Take a breath. Try again. There is never regret in trying, and we must not let the fact that this time it hasn't worked out stop us from going again. If something doesn't work out – bravo to us for giving it a whirl. Creativity involves taking risks. To not take those risks is to not create. And we're a long time dead.

The growing pains of failure are, admittedly, rarely fun. Some days it's really hard to swallow. It's tough when your gallery insists your bull-terrier is actually a sheep (yes, really …). I remember once when I was staying awhile in Rockbottomsville (see *Le Chien Noir*) listening to a radio interview with The Edge. In a voice of utmost gravity he confided: '*Getting to the good stuff is hard*'. I'm right behind you, Edge (from a slightly less world dominating vantage point), all the way. It's far from easy, and we have to allow for the 'not-so-good' stuff, and the turkeys, and the sheep along our way.

Overcoming Rejection: We never feel failure more directly than when we have suffered a rejection. It seems to crystallise the 'I'm just not good enough' in an internalised flashing neon sign. But consider this – so often it has really nothing to do with you at all. Really. In publishing matters, for example, you might write an absolute corker but if it doesn't fit the trend of the time, or you are not already a 'name' that a likely audience will recognise, it may not get picked up. A publishing house or production company needs to think about how it can work commercially for them, so unfortunately many beautiful writings and creative works will slip through. But go you for coming up with something beyond and novel – it certainly doesn't make it less brilliant, and you might just be ahead of the curve! It's a fact that acceptance rates by the top guns are low so isn't it just brilliant that we live in an age when we can self-publish – hard copy or digital. Rejection in industry matters is no longer the red light to Creatives it once was.

Besides, everyone gets rejected sometimes. Often it will be down to a mismatch – wrong audience/wrong in-tray. In cases where it *does* feel personal, I suggest you assume that the problem lies firmly with them, and not with you. Thank them kindly for their time, thank the Lord above and your lucky stars for weeding it out as that path wasn't your path, that gallery wall wasn't your gallery wall, that publishing house wasn't your publishing house, (that romantic charlatan wasn't your romantic charlatan) and that rejection saved you a whole heap of mileage. Back on your bike friend and pedal on.

A Pep Talk For Perfectionists: The ideal of perfection motivates and taunts us in equal parts. Use it, absolutely, as fuel to hit your high notes. Don't ever start your day aiming for mediocrity – this would be very wrong – but equally don't pitch your efforts against it as a be-all-and-end-all benchmark or you've lost before you've begun. Our creative wellsprings throw up chinks and spikes and dips and damaged dents and frayed endings and shining diamonds. All of these are ingredients in our unique creative expression and that is what makes it, and us, interesting.

If we really want technically 'perfect', we can go digital or AI – but where's the soul in that? Creativity is so much more. It is dependent upon artistic interpretation and it is from this individual human expression that I believe we are touched. It seems to me to be that human kink that strikes another human within, and that makes us feel human back.

If I don't convince you, The Boss might. The first time Bruce Springsteen heard the studio recording of his album Born to Run, he was, as the story goes, so unhappy with it, he threw the record in the swimming pool. All he could hear was what was wrong with it. Fortunately, his manager had a different perspective. '*Sometimes ... the things that are wrong with something are the things that make it great.*' It might help to contemplate that some 'flaws' are endearing, interesting and ultimately what makes work, work.

Striving for the 'perfect' is exhausting. Expecting it from your creativity is borderline delusional and if you've hung your hat on it, well you're in the wrong game. But we must never not strive to create to our utmost potential (that is compulsory) and pushing ourselves to our creative outer limits is vital too.

And on the way there, we stumble, we pause, we step backwards, we fail – we hate ourselves. It's all part of the artist's journey. But what do we do? WE GET UP AGAIN. '*Fail again. Fail better.*' Absolutely Mr. Beckett – you're on.

Some stumbler's self-soothing suggestions:

- On this path – the path not to perfection, but to achieving your maximum potential – allow yourself to feel your emotions. That energy in motion needs somewhere to go. If you're frustrated or sad, then scream or cry; it's all cool, groovy, more than necessary.

- Be nice to yourself. Again the stuff of clichés but I bet you forget it in the moment and get cross with yourself instead. The metaphorical donning of the cashmere wrap. We are sensitive creatures and when it's not working it hurts. (In tandem however, keep pushing yourself further than you think you can achieve! We may be sensitive, but we are also strong.)

- If you have to trash a morning's work, accept that that's ok – no time is time wasted if you have given yourself entirely to what you are doing. If you're pushing to create beyond where you've been before, some will fly, some will crash, some will bore. It's science, or Sod's law or something like that. Remember that Ernest Hemingway routinely deleted entire works and started over – to him it was part of the process. He apparently rewrote the ending to *A Farewell to Arms* 39 times. Lord above. Creativity is not a linear process. Each successful piece of work is not a spontaneous act of brilliance but a result of all the layers of feelings and learnings that have preceded its execution, and could only have manifested from the lessons that have gone before. Take a break, take the day off sometimes if you need to, and then back to where you left off. New dawn, new day, new dog (in my case) – new exciting potential.

- Do keep a check on your naughty inner critic and stay mindful of your self-criticism (as distinct from self-critiquing which is constructive and necessary). This is really important during learning curves and early drafts, especially when the creative chips are down. Even when you're awake to it, it can be difficult to change the record. Our ego gets involved and it all goes to pot. Be aware of self-berating thoughts. Push them back into the long grass, no place for those today.
- Work long term too on your self-compassion (this isn't just a girl thing, boys). It's a healthier more helpful in-built resource than self-confidence, which of course we all want but which can create inadvertent blindspots of your weak points when it gets out of hand. In engaging self-compassion you will look at yourself, objectively, but kindly, and make assessments from a more realistic starting and vantage point. You are not ignoring your limitations and shortcomings, but seeing how best to overcome them, dissolve them, build on them. It makes for a good sense of natural, sustainable and well-grounded confidence and that's the

way to go. Mindfully, realistically, but definitely with a healthy swagger on a good day too.

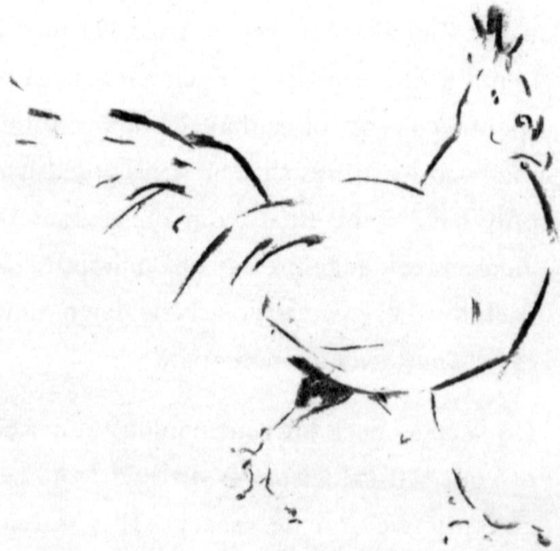

#RandomCockerelWithSwagger

- I'm going to throw in here the importance of maintaining a sense of self-identity beyond our creativity. This is especially true if we make our creative buddy our business. If we invest our entire sense of self in our work, we set ourselves up for difficult times. When our work hits some rough spots, inevitably, so do we. Author and spiritual teacher Dr. Wayne Dyer warned about equating our own self-worth with what we do. He put it this way: 'You aren't what you do. If you are what you do, then when you don't … you aren't.' 'I am because I write' – so if you don't write – 'you're not'? See how this works? Or doesn't.

Conclusion: Fortifying our sense of self is a lifetime's work. There is a yoga pose called Tadasana, the 'mountain pose', which is the essence of stability and foundation and the building block of most other poses. It commands a firm base and an upward reach – grounded and arising – roots and wings. When things feel wobbly we need to know our foundations are solid, so dig those roots deep. And wide.

Today's work may not be your best effort – Lord knows it may not even be instantly recognisable as the subject matter you intended. But work hard and with determination in what you do, and strive to be the best you can be, and then be grateful for where it takes you and the sheep – yes! – that you paint. (It did sell very quickly by the way… It must have been a nice sheep at least.)

Throughout your creative practice and your life, be capable of stepping back to look at both objectively. Engaging critical thinking is good (we must be kind to ourselves but not delusional) but acceptance when we've given our all is key. If I get to exhibition time and I've poured my heart and soul into the work and preparations – there is nothing more. Game set and match, I wish the paintings well, deep breath, smile on, curtains up.

x

SECTION VI: BREAK COVER

By this point you have amassed a magnificent range of self-assisting ninja moves all under one roof. Go you. There will still be clouds – that's life – but you know you can push on up through them. If you have (and I really hope you do) dreams of shooting skywards, this section is designed to champion you on.

So, dear Creative, are you ready to show the world what you can do? If you are considering tipping the balance of your work life into your chosen creative practice, I'm so pleased you're embracing it seriously. I'm 100 per cent behind the school of doing what you really want to do and giving it your all. As well as being a soul fulfilling life, the creative path can also be a truly rewarding career. However, these are precarious times and life asks a lot of us (not least financially) so the degree to which you make your art your life is something only you can decide.

I hope this section will help you in assessing if it is the right *career* path for you. If you do decide to go full-on commercially 'in' you will need a de-risking process and pragmatic strategy underpinning your fabulous dreams. **Chapter 16** looks at placing this important part of your life in your centre stage and the experience I had in doing so. **Chapter 17** outlines your due diligence to evaluate how that centre stage might look for you.

Three, two, one …

Chapter 16

GOING NATIVE CREATIVE

'Unfurl yourself into the grace of beginning
That is at one with your life's desire.
Awaken your spirit to adventure'

For a New Beginning
— John O'Donohue —
Poet

Immersing yourself fully into your creativity is an exciting and potentially life-changing progression. Romantic me is saying 'go for it'; sensible me is saying I've been blinded by romance before, but I still believe in a really good match. If your reality allows and your gut says 'yes I'm in' and you sleep on it some and it's still giving you the thumbs up – well then, a feisty foot forward friends.

If you are being employed to use your creativity, I think you've hit the jackpot – a win-win of security and satisfaction. If you need to work part-time while growing your skills until the maths work out, this can be really good too. One foot on shore while pushing your budding career boat out can give you the stability you need to succeed. If this is the case,

I strongly urge you not to rush the transition. At times – especially in the early stages – the reality of needing to rely on our work for our bread and butter can be really quite overwhelming. Sometimes you will create at your best while toggling between the two. We need to protect our sense of self and wellbeing always, not least to come up with great art!

Having said that, I'm a mighty believer in leaps of faith combined, always, with hard graft. If we work tenaciously and consistently from an open heart in our creative calling we're bound to produce something good. And if we truly believe in it, the right audience, when we find it, is bound to believe in it too. You need to have an inner belief in what you are doing, otherwise it's impossible to maintain your momentum in the quieter times. (However, if lack of self-belief stopped all Creatives from doing their thing there would scarcely be a piece of art out there. Self-doubt and self-questioning are, as we know, never far from the artist's door.)

My Jump

When I took my jump from corporate to creative I knew in my heart that there were other avenues in life I needed to explore. This winking silver lining of the unexpected freedom that had landed in my lap – aged 35, separated, no children, only myself in practical terms to look after – gave me the now-or-never impetus to take the chance. I started investigating studios, and what I might do when I got there. I got a job working in the beautiful Sladmore sculpture gallery in London, four days a week, and played hooky from real life the remaining three, to see what I could make of my art.

Two years later I borrowed some money to host a short solo show in Mayfair of my charcoal drawings. This was when my art was still a relatively new friend: we were only getting to know each other but so far it was going well. I had built up a body of work that I believed in, and I needed to see if anyone else did too. I included some bronze sculpture I had begun working on in my kitchen when I was married, playing with plasticine instead of pulling dinner together; in retrospect I really wasn't great wife material at all. The reaction to the show was heart-warmingly supportive and it gave me the courage to jump. A reshuffle of my work life thereafter allowed a part-time office job to support my painting days as I worked towards a bigger more colourful gathering. My Rogues Gallery exhibition four years later gave me my roots and my wings and since then (nine years on, and counting) I have painted full-on, full-time.

Deciding to go native creative was much like deciding to get married. I find decisions regarding serious commitments less than easy to take and am prone to long stints on the fence. You can sit indefinitely and weigh it all up but then you must ask yourself the question: '*How would I feel if I decided not to follow my heart's desire?*' Or: '*How would I feel if I went through life without following my artistic calling?*' For me, for both, regret, regret, regret, and we know how we feel about that.

Some Starting Block Thoughts:

- There is always a shift in dynamic when courtship becomes full-blown commitment. Be aware of this so as not to be spooked when you decide your art will be your breadwinner as well as your love.
- There may also be a shift in direction to consider if you are depending solely on the income from your art. You may need to tailor your creative output to what people will respond to, rather than following your pure artistic calling. Essentially, you will have to think commercially. You may, however, be lucky enough to find that the commercial world supports your natural flow from the outset – in which case, hooray! Listen to your audience, as well as your authentic self, is what I'm saying.

- In being a full-on commercial Creative, and thereby binding yourself to the consideration of others, you can be in danger of losing that very freedom we find when we lose ourselves in our work. Before jumping, ask yourself what elements of your work have been well received to date, and can you follow on in that vein going forward? What do you do naturally (i.e. sustainably) well, that people respond to? You can be massively talented but if it doesn't connect to your audience you won't be able to pay the bills. I don't want you to be artistically fulfilled but starving. Equally, nor will you thrive if you *only* dance for the creative piper. Balance wisely friends.
- Become more familiar with your own creative scene and take in a bit of artistic gallivanting early on. Not only is it so lovely to meet others in your boat, but also you will learn more about what is current and effective in terms of various routes to market (you now *need* a market) taken by your peers. In early days, throw your hat in the ring for events, gatherings and festivals that pertain to your art; at worst you'll have an interesting encounter with fellow tribesmen, and some serendipitous encounters might just give you a little leg-up in starting out.
- You will need stamina. Stamina for when the editing process begins – you thought when you wrote a book the hard work was done – for commercial purposes this is when the hard work begins! I had read that the editing process takes four times longer than the writing process; I thought – *who needs so much editing?* (Aaaand … Take 6 …) And when working to commission you might be delighted with what you deliver but the heart sinks when they see it differently and editing is asked for. Experience shows that once you change one thing the rest then requires tweaking in support/sympathy. Your compositions are the sum

of their individual and important separate parts. This can be heart-breaking and art breaking. Once you are being paid to deliver it becomes what the client sees more than what you see. Sorry to be depressing but I have to flag this up. Stamina peeps.

- You must take the time you require to develop your skills so that you are robust enough when you decide you want to lean on them. The build-up to your best might take longer than you estimate – Malcolm Gladwell's 10,000 hours theory isn't too far off to my mind. He popularised the idea that if you practise one skill for 10,000 hours, you'll have a good chance of becoming an expert at it. Michelangelo was said to say: *'If people know how hard I worked to get my mastery, it wouldn't seem so wonderful at all.'* If the great man himself had to put the hours in, we most certainly do.

- On that note – even when you have all the skills you need, don't underestimate the graft that being a career Creative involves. It is hard, HARD work to sustain being a fulfilled creative. You will have to roll up your sleeves. 90 per cent of what you do will not feel like you are being kissed by stardust. '*Inspiration exists*', as Picasso put it, '*but it has to find you working*'.

Some More Thoughts:
The best way to proceed at this point is to take the temperature of how your work is received. Start putting your talented toes in the water:

- Obviously begin to show your work through digital platforms – Chapter 19 will help you out here.

- To gauge initial reactions consider collaborating in an exhibition or performance. Sharing costs and pooling address books and audiences is an obvious way to begin. It eases the financial pressure, broadens your reach and makes it far less totally terrifying. If promoting the event sounds equally terrifying Chapter 18 will help you on this.

- When first seeking an outlet or representation for your work, look to others' work in a similar genre and see how it's made its way out to the world. Agents/publicists/producers/galleries will all have specific expertise and contacts in their niche fields. It is so much better for everybody when your wares and genius are pitched to the right person or lands in the most conducive-to-success intray possible. If you research and plan strategically the path ahead for your work, you'll find most people really helpful in guiding you along the way.

- Consider competitions and awards – they are a great way to get feedback, experience and build up your creative CV. Get googling. For example: 'writing competition non-fiction' or 'nautical painting competition', which will take you to the prizewinning sections of relevant societies and organisations. Ditto for industry awards – search your metier: 'young musician awards' or 'awards young designers' may give you the gateway to the kudos you need. There is zero downside in taking part and some great recognition and financial rewards to be had. And you are igniting your own PR. Some of my brave friends have found themselves on the Sky artist of the year series and it never hasn't done them the world of good. This is slightly the deep-end option – you can start more regional before world domination if that's more your thinking right now. But don't rule out the major networks when you're ready!

- I haven't yet mentioned the bible for writers. This would be the blessing that is *The Writers' and Artists' Yearbook* (updated annually), and its relevance to your creative expression in a professional context cannot be expressed sufficiently here. It is indispensable for authors but a benevolent tome for illustrators, painters and photographers too. (There's even a brilliant basic lowdown included on the taxing matters of tax.) For those who have taken, or are considering taking, the full immersion into the creative calling this will hold your hand on the diving board and you'll have found a trusty friend for life.

If you haven't started out as an artist, career lane switches to follow the hearts call are commonplace in Creativeland. Christian Dior studied to be a diplomat before finding his fashion-house fame. Sir Tim Rice left the law for his lyrics. Lewis Carroll was a mathematician and Haruki Murakami was a jazz club owner, before each followed their respective literary dreams. These are just a scattering across the successful lane switch spectrum but they might inspire.

If I'm playing devil's advocate, however, remember too that some of the great romances are that because they remained as a love affair/a forever crush/a soulmate never meant for the corsets and confines of marriage – and that's all exquisite too. Being a dedicated, progressing, Creative doesn't necessarily need to be career changing and there is much to be said for keeping your art as your joy, and still sharing it with the world.

To decide what's right for you, you need to investigate, forensically, how it is likely to look in practise. The following chapter should help you. Belts, braces and business beginnings, read on…

Chapter 17

GOING COMMERCIAL CREATIVE

'When you see someone putting on his Big Boots, you can be pretty sure that an Adventure is going to happen.'

— A.A. Milne —
Winnie-the-Pooh

When you're living your best life, sometimes you've just got to go all in. But you should first understand some business basics of a life in the creative arts. The intricate ins and outs are the subject for another book – they are too many and too metier specific to cover in sufficient detail here. Instead I am going to highlight what you need to consider when you're standing at the split path – Creatives, this way … Sensibles, the other … Let's pick up a few stones from the Sensibles' path to help us over some puddles which lurk down the Creatives' way:

Be Real

Be The Business

Be The Boss

Be Legally Savvy

Be Out There

Be In Touch.

Be Real

No mon no fun. This is about *your* personal circumstances and you'll need to make a clear-headed assessment of your finances. Look at all your likely outlays balanced against your income, both current and realistically potential. Get down to it with a spreadsheet. Make sure that all your potential costs have been factored in. This means setting out your likely costs of production, and your overheads (rent, insurance, IT, accounting fees etc.). Included in these overheads will be the costs of getting your work to market. Agents acting on your behalf will charge (often substantial) commission; if going solo you will pay for self-publishing/self-production/self-showcasing, as your creative work requires.

This is not a formulaic exercise – these are your needs and your reality. Write down too if you need to set aside money for childcare/tax/therapy(!), and a bit extra for the fun fund and the sink fund too. Talk it through with a friendly accountant. The last thing I want is to be a drag on your adrenaline here but financial stress on top of creative stress can really take its toll.

Pricing your work: Deciding on a price point – adequate to cover your time and your costs, enough to make you some profit, but not so much to turn off potential buyers – is easier said than done. You have to reassess your hobby as your revenue source (hat-switch), and you have to be pragmatic. If you can't eat, you can't create. Simple as.

- Take a look at your hours put in, to work put out. Early in your career, and even not so early, it is likely you are working hard at below the minimum wage. Sometimes this is a hit we take for the bigger picture and is a good reason to not rush transitions. This can't work in the long run, however, so as you get going you need to work out how many hours a typical project will likely take you.
- You also need to factor in your expertise. This is a variable that will rise in the eyes of your audience as your reputation and your accolades/Booker prizes/Grammys grow!
- When you have considered all costs to produce your work, then your prices must be balanced against what the market can stand, i.e. what your likely clients will be happy to pay. Investigate the competition. What are your contemporaries in your field charging? Consider their experience, time spent building up their following, the support they have gained from agents/others respected in the field and their 'special something'. (While investigating, keep in mind what you do differently to them – you want to distinguish yourself in some capacity – identify your 'special something' here too.)
- Having done all the homework, I still rely hugely on my gut barometer to help me decide what to charge for my artwork. Something in me tells me what it's worth me selling it for – below which I would rather keep it (although purist price setters will baulk at this and it doesn't pay for my next roll of linen).
- If you are reluctant to charge properly (or at all) for what you do, think of all the hours it took you to be the talented Creative you now are. Consider all the hours that got you to here – for many it started half a lifetime ago, or more. Not that you will charge the client for this but remember it in establishing your worth.

Silence the embarrassed voice in your head, *'this is just me doing what I love so I can't possibly charge you – have it for free!'* Nooooo...! What you are bringing to the table/easel/dancefloor now is only possible because of all the sweat, tears and gruelling hours that went down before. Don't undersell yourself, and do believe in your worth.

- Bear in mind that once you begin you can never drop your (like for like) prices as this would do a major disservice to those who invested and believed in you in the early days. Of course you might have a sale or give a discount to a good client but the retail price must be steadfast, or up. Early on you will want to make your work affordable to grow a following, and then bring people with you as you grow. This is all to be balanced against what makes it work for you. There is little satisfaction in following your creative calling if it will leave you feeling anxious and broke.

Making it work: If the costs of your commercial creative practice are feeling prohibitive to begin with – don't let this in itself stop you. Remember how resourceful and imaginative we Creatives are? Approach it practically:

- **Bridging your earnings**: I am totally in favour of having a part time job for fiscal, social and mental health reasons. Supplementing your income can be vital to your productivity (and your larder). Please consider this seriously. Look at ways you can continue to earn while you get established, preferably with part-time employment relevant to your own creative discipline. Gaining industry experience is never not a good thing. Usually you can still be in a contract of employment with an organisation or a company, and be self-employed at the same time with income generated from your art. I'm all for mixing it up between the two. Just be aware, however, how they dovetail – check your contracts for restrictive clauses, and anything that might result in the copyright in your freelance/own creative work being assigned to your employer, pertinent where you are employed using your creativity (e.g. graphic designing, content writing, illustrating). Your intellectual property can be your most valuable asset (see below).

- **Supporting your earnings**: Beyond the safety net of an employment contract, consider the following too:

    - Sharing workspaces with other Creatives – you can do this by finding a room in an artist's studio community or joining a coworking space. It saves on outgoings, pools resources, and taps you into a like-minded community where creative sparks can fly.

    - Crowdfunding is an option if you need a big injection to get a creative project off the ground. From big fish to niche platforms – look into Kickstarter, Indiegogo, Patreon, Unbound, Artshare etc. (this area is developing all the time).

    - Take time too to look into grants, funding, awards, residencies, bursaries – they are there, just waiting for you to research them. Do take a look at the suggested websites to follow.

    - Ask yourself what you do that others might need in a happy exchange for the services they could provide to your business? Their illustrations for your photography? Their copywriting for your video making? Their dog portrait for your marketing?! Think good old-fashioned swapping of desirable skills – again, I know you have them.

- **Even more earnings ...** Have in mind that once you are up and running you might diversify your revenue streams in relation to your art. Consider early on how you can have an income from multiple sources. To kick-start your thinking:
    - Private tutorials/group lessons. You might need a certain amount of established recognition for this one, depending on the calibre of the institution, but equally all teachers start somewhere.
    - Copywriting/editing/creative writing workshops.
    - Designing/illustrating (if considering illustration, check out www.theaoi.com – great for awards too – and pick up *Artist's and Illustrator's magazine*).
    - Organising an exhibition is an obvious starting point, as is taking on commissions – but be warned these might come with a toll.
    - Auctions of work through your website between big events.
    - A print run of your favourite or most popular works/ limited editions of cast bronzes if sculpting (remember your artist's copy).
    - Licensing your work (although note the lawyery points which I touch on later in this chapter).

Finances and circumstances in order (or at least reviewed), you now need to start to see your art baby as your art business. Pull back to take a helicopter view.

Be The Business

Put your business hat on top of your creative hat and take a look at your own Alan-Sugar-self from above. Ideally, you need a mentor to best do this, or at least a sensible pal. Either way, toss your budding business ideas around with someone you trust.

If you feel initially daunted by the concept of your creativity as a business, pull back again and break it down. Just have your short-term goals in place all dotting a steady map towards your long-term ideal. Long-term vision, if starting as a business, is important – this isn't a 'let's see how we go lads' scenario. Work out where you're going and then get organised to get there.

Plan plan plan: Write up a basic business plan or at the very least a realistic action plan. You need to see things in black and white to make clear judgement calls. Fundamental is knowing who your clients/audience are going to be, how to connect with them, and how to *keep* connecting. Building on this, give some thought to how and where you might best and most profitably showcase your work.

While you'd expect me to encourage you to plan ahead (do!), as you know I'm all for planning backwards too. What I mean by this is that you set your vision *out there* on a realistic end point, and then trace your steps backwards to where you are now. This way you can plan what needs to be done, and when, so you get to the destination, intact, ready, and on time. Writers will know more about this than others – the power of a plot line is well understood in their world. Musicians and visual artists might be a bit more 'free range' here! This particular artist took guidance from a writer well versed in the art of planning backwards – on the back of a paper napkin in a Pret a Manger on Piccadilly after an inspiring visit to the Royal Academy Summer Exhibition. (I told you it was good to get *out there.*)

For what it's worth, here's what we came up with:

If planning an exhibition, you need to work out what you need to earn to make it work and worth your while. What 'worth your while' is might be financial bounty, great PR, or just a solid stepping-stone in your career. Factor in the number of pieces that you need, of varying sizes and price points, showcasing what you do. Then work backwards on a realistic time frame you need to complete the work (including framing etc.). This allows you to calculate how you might best work to maximum efficiency (perhaps two big ones on the go over three months with six smaller ones to be completed at the same time, if working that way works for you).

Basically – have a linear methodology to support your end goal and your very best intuitive own-coach way of getting there. This is your business, your work, your plan.

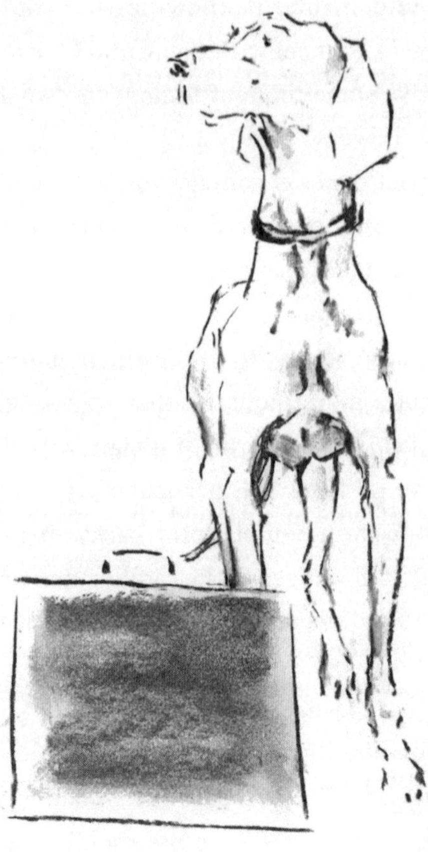

Get organised: I've got to state the obvious – get organised. That's the real secret of being in charge of your own successful business – kick the artist stereotype and shock your creative siblings – get your little desk ducks in a row:

- **£££**: If you take the leap it will really help to get yourself a good invoicing system. Xero/Quickbooks/Wave/Invoice Home or another accounting system, so it's all transparent and easy and doesn't floor you when it comes to self-assessment. You need to be aware of what goes out and what comes in and where you stand at all times – no room for surprises here.
- **www.**: Use the technology we are lucky enough to have at our fingertips. Get your website domain name and all online handles sorted early doors. Even this dinosaur had to get with it web-wise.
- Get your mailing list in order. We should ideally be building up our mailing lists from the moment we make our first plasticine and matchstick porcupine, or soon thereafter. This is your starting audience and the beginning point for your 'collector relations' too. (And yes, there's the danger that it makes us very annoying people, but needs sort of must.) More later on keeping things legal when handling people's contact details.
- Keep note too of who mentioned they might be interested in what, who introduced you, when, where etc. One day you might have magnificently captured a certain landscape, or hit upon the perfect score for the next award-winning drama, and be scratching your head as to who wanted it, or how you met them. (If you're contacting somebody out of the blue some time after you've met them, putting your earlier meeting in context is essential.)

- If you're a visual artist, get your images in order. This is key from the first piece you are proud of. I kicked myself I didn't invest in a decent camera or work with a professional photographer early on – some of my favourite pieces lurk on my laptop only as a grainy reminder that I should have recorded them differently. They might have made a lovely print run or at least good promotional starting points – don't miss a trick like I did. Images, images, images – of everything – they are your currency. And a heads-up when it comes to doing your PR – you should have your images saved (under names or captions, not numbers) as jpegs (not PDFs) and ready to send in low res with a follow up high res (minimum 300 dpi) thereafter.
- Other artists need to be stage ready too. Have your demos/ portfolios/recordings ready at the push of a button. Attention spans are limited – if someone is interested, show them straight away how rightly placed their interest is. Have them of high quality, and ready, right now. You don't want to keep Messrs Saatchi, Sony or Spielberg waiting when they're knocking on your door.
- Pedantic yes, but record everything. Besides keeping financial records in order (generally six years back for tax assessment purposes in the UK, seven years in Ireland) you should have systems for all of the above.

Be the Boss

Few of us understand what going solo really means when we're starting our journey – and the lessons can be hard learned when we supplement hope for homework. Here are some being the boss basics:

Self-employment: It can be a shock to realise that self-employment isn't all about the freedom to create. You have a few civic obligations too – most notably sorting out your tax status and the consequences thereof. You don't want to fall at the first hurdle beneath tax jargon, contributions due and insurance (of your work/studio/goods in transit, and potentially public liability insurance too). You need to know what being self-employed really means, what you need to pay, when, and what you will be responsible for. Grown-up style.

The first port of call when considering being self-employed is www.gov.uk in the UK and www.revenue.ie in Ireland. There is lots of good info and I've always found a patient voice at the end of the line to help. Both jurisdictions require you to register as self-employed when you start earning money from your creative work through sales or other freelance opportunities. The level of income at which this obligation kicks in differs, and is subject to annual change, so bear it in mind and research the amount for your own tax year.

Taxes: You will need to submit your tax return by, at the latest, online, 31 January in the UK and within weeks (it changes annually) of 31 October in Ireland for the previous tax year. If you can't face doing it yourself and you have the funds to outsource it, do exactly that. Bear in mind however that even if employing a professional, you will need to provide them with ALL the relevant information. They will tell you to keep records of EVERYTHING. There are things you didn't know you could expense or apportion to expenses, depending on how they fall between your personal and professional use. When you are self-employed you pay income tax on your profits and not on your total income, i.e. your total income minus your business expenses, so when you start working for yourself this will really help the maths work. Keep records of every last tuppence.

I'm not going to go into the details of income tax, tax allowances, tax rates, etc. – life is too short, and anyway, the details are ever changing. Hop online and go straight to the horse's mouth – your country's revenue site. Look for all information pertaining to self-employment, and have a quick scout around to see if there is ever any special treatment awarded to Creatives. (In Ireland, for instance, the Artists' Tax exemption helps those self-employed in the creative arts.)

To do yourself, delegate or upskill?: If you are going to be your own boss you need to be real about what you're naturally good at and what you'd do best to delegate. Trying to do everything is a false economy. In this assessment consider too what you could be good at if you give yourself half a chance, and what might be worth your while learning. I got my head around building my own websites on Squarespace and working with Pixelmator so that I could show my work effectively. My sister is a whizz on Wix and Canva – divide and conquer! (She can help you too if you need her – www.elfmedia.ie.) I'm all for trying to get geeky if it saves me outlay and helps what I do. But if it's going to be an ongoing battle and drains your precious creative hours, get someone to do it for you. Again, I ask on artists forums for recommendations and have a great little self-employed support team for when my will to webwork wanes. (Fiverr and Upwork are excellent resources here.) If you want to get your skills up and wonder how you could be *even* better at this being-the-boss lark, platforms like Skillshare, Udemy and of course YouTube are there to teach you anything you need to know.

At this point – you have done your own cost interrogation, you have a plan and you have a basic understanding of what being self-employed might look like for you. And your friendly accountant might have earned himself a sketch, a scotch or a stilton by now. It is sometimes worth having a friendly lawyer on your contact lists too, but in the meantime …

Be Legally Savvy

Small print matters.

If you have an agent (or a recording company or a publishing house or a gallery) in the wings – this is fabulous. But a word here on the ancillary contracts – keep those antennae up. I learned this the hard way, and I'm a qualified solicitor. Get it agreed, and get it in writing. (It's clichéd, yes, but vital.)

Here are some basic legal heads-up, so you don't get tripped up early on (or ever) and to help you to avoid avoidable pitfalls in protecting you, your reputation and your precious work:

Contracts: If you are agreeing to any type of commercial or contractual arrangement, there is no creative work that you do that isn't worthy of protecting with basic agreement formulas that will show your work, your client, and yourself the respect all three of you deserve. It also guarantees subsequent remuneration where it is wholly and fully due. Here's a sixty second whirlwind around contracts:

- The main rule for contracts is that everyone should know where everyone stands – who is responsible for what and the terms under which you are engaging. Who, what, when, how and the bottom-line dollar. The most important of these (after 'How Much?') are the 'What Ifs'. Make sure your written agreement tells the full story, get those deets and worst-case play outs down. What if Covid stops the show? What if the venue burns down the day before? What if they delay the payment? Imagine every (realistic) scenario, and provide for it in the contract. Keeping it simple is fine but keep it in writing. Read and understand everything before signing – it's so exciting to get your work on a gallery wall or with a publishing house or recording studio, but only if it's working in your interests – eyes open. Even the small print – I'm afraid so.

- If you are freelance/self-employed make sure the contracts you sign are not 'contracts for employment' or you may find yourself exposed to tax or copyright issues (more on copyright and contracts below).
- Matters can be signed off digitally if necessary, and aptly these days with apps such as Hello Sign or any of its equivalents (Electronic signing is legally binding in Ireland, UK and US amongst other jurisdictions – check this if a contract party is beyond these areas).
- Before agreeing the percentage commission, be aware of the financial consequences of VAT/your agent's discounts/extra expenses on you. Early on, I failed to factor in that signing for a gallery to take 45% meant 45% plus their sales tax. While I'm on this topic, and at the risk of getting specific for artists in my own field – most galleries will be registered for VAT, while fledgling artists won't. Check this in your own field and understand that you might be receiving less for your work than you were expecting. Some galleries will add sales tax on top of the total sale price. You need to be clear what you need to get paid for your work to make it worth selling through an agent or a gallery. Discuss framing costs (or other relevant output) from the outset. Generally, the framing costs are with the artist but you might negotiate that gallery commission is charged net of your framing costs, or they might offer to pay half. Remember – everything is negotiable. Agree early on about discounts they will offer on your work – galleries are sometimes willing to give 10–15% to good clients or for multiple purchases (with only one of them yours). All these things need to be worked out from the start. If

you are leaving work with them, sign and keep copies of a delivery (or a consignment – depending on the arrangement) note. It will detail particular works and will be your proof of title in case of mis-memories/misplacements/liquidation/insurance claims.

- If you do find yourself early on being offered a contract and are tempted – because, who wouldn't be? – a word of advice: don't fall over yourself to please. This is a business agreement – TREAT IT AS SUCH. My next embarrassment: being so overwhelmed with gratitude that *somebody wanted to show my work!*, I signed up to onerous clauses that weren't being imposed on the other artists showing through this agent. Take off your self-effacing blinkers and get with the commercial programme. Talk to contemporaries who have representation. Know what the general form is. Again – don't be proud and don't be younger me.

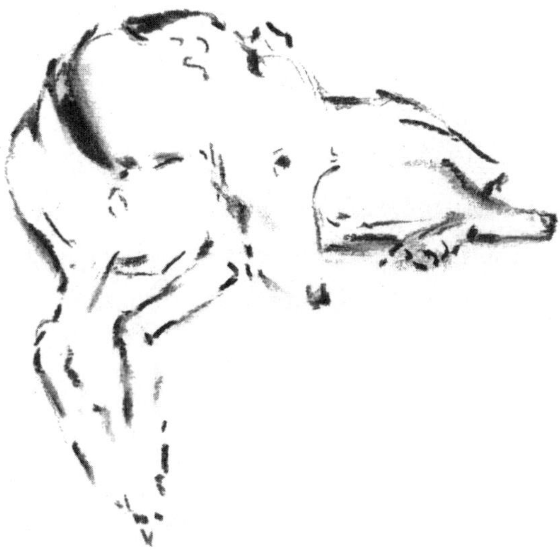

Having said all of this … it can be worth being flexible if the prestige of being associated with their stable will benefit your standing as an artist. Equally, factor in the marketing they do of you and your work – in my field at art fairs, to their clients and on the art scene as a whole. This can be alien and cringe territory for an artist – self-promotion is a really tricky tight rope to negotiate and one that generally leaves us blushing, inept or giving our work away at prices we later regret and can ill afford. More than that, when you sometimes find this flying solo business testing, it is really lovely having a good working relationship that benefits you both. I have had that too and it's fabulous. It's a balance to be struck between you with everyone's interests looked after, and input appreciated on all sides. Get it right (in writing!) for a healthy and happy long-term relationship to unfold where both parties feel valued, and expectations are fulfilled.

Overall, just make sure that you're on board with the story being told by the document you're signing. If a formal contract for any reason has not yet been signed, at the very least always be able to refer to an exchange of emails agreeing to all the important terms of the arrangement. And remember to advocate – for yourself and for your art.

Intellectual Property: You will need to become familiar with some aspects of IP, especially Copyright, but also Licensing, Moral Rights and, as you progress, Artists Resale Rights too. In a nutshell your IP rights exist to protect the intangible elements to your physical creative work, i.e.: the thought process/skill/unique combinations in use of design elements involved etc. These can all constitute a valuable asset beyond the physical artwork itself.

- **Copyright**: Generally speaking, copyright arises automatically and stays with you as the creator of an original work, once that work is sold (although there are exceptions to this – see below). It gives you, as the creator, ownership of the legal rights to control and protect the use of your original works. Basically it constitutes the right to reproduce a piece of work anytime, anywhere, for the creator's lifetime plus 70 years (or so – depending on the country and the type of work) and therefore protects your work from being copied without permission. You can perform, show, play, broadcast or adapt your work however you like. **Be very reluctant to let copyright go – think 'exclusive license' rather than 'assignment/transfer', always.**

To establish parentage of your work, you can use the copyright symbol '©', followed by your name and year of origin. You can send your solicitor a copy (musicians can include an audio recording) or you can send it by recorded post to yourself with your signature across the seal and keep it unopened as proof. (There is less need for either these days as our tech history make dating work possible in most cases but if you want belt and braces do.) If you're worried about illegal use of your images, publish them online in low res only or with a watermark running through. Otherwise embed your information into the metadata (not entirely theft-proof), or use invisible barcoding – research how these might work for you.

If you are a freelancer, be aware that there's a glaring exception to the copyright rule. Where original work is created in the course of employment, by an employee as part of their job (e.g. a graphic designer designing within a company) copyright will automatically become the property of the employer. If you are a freelance artist working on commission, you will retain your own copyright unless you contractually agree otherwise. READ THE SMALL PRINT. It is very common for freelancing or consultancy contracts to remove copyright from the creators.

- **Licensing your work**: A big benefit to retaining your intellectual property rights is the ability to increase your revenue through licensing or merchandising agreements. If you are considering granting a licence do check contracts thoroughly for definitions of 'usage'. This will determine where and how your work will be shared or shown. Licences can be 'exclusive', 'sole' or 'non-exclusive'; a sole licence – where only one person can use your work – is obviously more valuable than non-exclusive. Look out for exclusive licences however as these exclude you – the creator – from using your work as long as the licence is in place. You might be OK with that, if the price is right, but be sure to know what you are agreeing to. Irrespective of the exclusivity, you should be remunerated according to the extent of use in terms of time, territory and media. Words like 'global', 'worldwide', 'irrevocable', and 'in perpetuity' are a big deal and should be considered very carefully. Also look to any 'restrictive clauses' proposed – a licensee may wish to stop you licensing to a direct competitor whereas they may not have an issue with you licensing to different types of businesses. Just be aware.

  I would strongly urge you to always lean towards 'licence' and not 'assignment' or 'transfer' – both are tantamount to selling your copyright, which means you have no control over the way in which your creative work is used in the future. Licensing on the other hand can be conducted on very mutually beneficial and flexible terms. The benefits are that you retain your rights but give another party permission to use your work in a manner that is agreeable to you, on your terms. Don't settle for anything less.

- **Moral rights**: These are a bundle of personal rights which are yours for the same period as copyright. They include your right to be identified as the creator of a work, and your right to object to derogatory treatment of your work. These rights remain yours even if you no longer own the copyright in your work. This means that they cannot be assigned to anyone else but – watch out for this – they can be waived in a contract so look out for a 'waiver of moral rights' term. It's a no-no. Keep them if you can, and if you do have to waive them you might negotiate a higher fee for this.

- **Artist's Resale Rights**: As your career progresses you may want to get familiar with the ARR, or '*droit de suite*'. These rights give the creators of qualifying original works of art (graphic works, paintings, sculptures and collages) the right to a royalty when their work is resold through a 'qualifying intermediary' in qualifying territories in the EU and the UK. They apply to living artists (and more recently they also apply to their heirs).

- **Trademark protection**: It might not be for everyone, but many Creatives (musicians in particular) do register their names as trademarks. A registered trademark prevents others from providing the same or similar goods and services under your name. Without a trademark you can still object to people passing off your work as theirs using the law of – you guessed it – passing off. But to win a passing off claim the onus is on you to prove the extent of your reputation, that deception is taking place and that you are suffering damage as a result. It's all a lot more straightforward if you have a registered trademark. Registering a UK trademark costs start from £170, Irish trademarks are available from €70. If someone else is covering the cost for you, make sure that you are named as the owner of the trademark. And never sell your trademark rights unless you have no intention of creating under that name again. Designers from Elizabeth Emanuel to Karen Millen have been stung by that one.

All of these are dealt with comprehensively on websites I will detail at the end of this chapter. (Also check out www.honeycomb.law – creative law for creative people – if you need help in this field.) The IP offices in your jurisdiction will help you too.

Know your 'Ps' from your 'Ts and Cs': One last thing – make sure your website small print is in good order – Privacy Policy, Cookie Policy, and Terms and Conditions of trade. There are some great independent and affordable legal consultants who help freelancers and self-employeds specifically with these for a one-off fee. Thereafter make sure that your emailing shenanigans are GDPR compliant, i.e. running your mailing list so that you are landing in inboxes that have opted in to welcoming you there.

The 2016 General Data Protection Regulation guidelines are in charge here. At the time of writing there is an unstable (confused?) elephant in the room called Brexit. The data protection laws stem from EU regulation. For the time being UK law (the amended Data Protection Act 1998) is in line with GDPR but, while that could change, it isn't likely to in the very near future. In any event, the implemented regulations cover the personal data of all EU citizens, no matter where they are in the world, and your email list will most likely include non-British citizens in these days of global easy comms. They also provide a framework of good practice that basically won't irritate unnecessarily so it's worth the effort to get your comms GDPR compliant. You might have a quick google around the subject and if in doubt that friendly lawyer for small businesses will check over your wording so you're good to go.

Be Out There

(In Twofold – Your Work and You)

Your Work: The previous chapter saw you bravely beginning to see how your work goes down beyond the rose-tints of your support team/puppy/lover. This will help you decide if your creativity in its current form has 'commercial legs'. If you are now going to seek a dream investor in your chosen art field (be it agent/producer/gallery/publisher/choreographer), you will need to show them what a very good decision investing in you would be.

Begin by establishing yourself in your field to the degree that you are able – everyone starts somewhere. It might be gigging in a local library, pub or café, performance artistry in Covent Garden (outside, not necessarily inside, the Opera House), or busking on Grafton Street (remember the power of a video going viral... ask along a friend handy with a phone). Likewise, a writer can launch a career by writing a blog or starting a podcast – you just need to gather an interested following. You'll be a long time waiting for the white knight to come knocking on your door (especially if he doesn't know you exist) – we have to bring our front door to him.

Create your own showtime ... I loved running my own exhibition, accountable only to my work and to me. It's a great opportunity to show who you really are in your own independent style and invite those potential future business partners along. I am going to share with you a few things I learned. Whatever your medium, if you decide to run your own show, some of these pointers should help you too – adapt as necessary:

- It doesn't need to run for a long time – spend money on a good location (for credibility and footfall) and show for a shorter time if rent is prohibitive. Two good parties and some follow up days for subsequent sales should give you a very good run. Date-wise

I find that May and November (to early December) tend to work well.

- To help with a top location, you might approach a sponsor? This could also alleviate the bar bill if you can get a drinks sponsorship, or reduce the cost of catalogue production should you credit them in it. Think outside the box – offer a corporate evening's viewing for their client entertainment? Think who might be a good fit and how this could work for all.

- The all-important PR. Create a buzz before and after your event, not only on social media, but through other channels too. You need to make a list really early on of where you would love a mention, and approach them well in advance with a good image and tempting copy. Get online and offline publication lead times diarised and get any good contacts you have on board early. Time flies when you have your head in your art getting ready for a show – this needs to be a priority as lead times can be six months or more. More on this in Chapter 18.

- For the night itself, you might be lucky to find someone to send a photographer but you will need your own photographer lined up too. Share the buzz! It's great to have some good publicity shots of you doing your thing ready to roll.

- Your invitations are worth spending money on. Remember that a lovely invitation will sit on mantelpieces throughout the land – who knows how many pairs of eyes could see them? Use a strong image and make it top quality and a decent size.

- Have the premises and work insured (and remember goods in-transit insurance too.) For art on walls, try to find a delivery company which is a hanging company as well – you will have minimal hours to make those walls sing as in a top-notch venue the previous gig might have left only hours before.

- Spend money on good presentation. In the visual arts it is everything. GET YOUR LIGHTING RIGHT. I can't stress this enough – I got it wrong on a recent occasion and my dogs and I regretted it terribly. Don't be (not so younger) me.
- Get your cashpoint/payment apps working and sales forms at the ready for easy complete payment and delivery details for when the rush comes on…
- Be as good a host as you are an artist. To do this have a really good little team in place (barmen vital – and a great friend/sibling/PA managing sales) so that you can mix and talk and engage with those who have made the effort to be there.
- Light a candle. I find prayers and lime blossom go a long way in high octane times.
- Breathe. I have to step outside to regroup myself at moments – and also to get myself back into the 'now' so that I can remember to enjoy this terrifying trip!
- No need for eats – it is not a food fest but an art fest. But definitely pour decent drink – those who are good enough to come and support you really deserve it. I sold two paintings to a lovely client who said it was because I had his favourite wine (and I thought it was that my little dachshunds were irresistible).
- In a recent collaborative exhibition with two wonderful artists, we ran an evening amongst the art to give an Artist's Talk. One showed us his clever behind the scenes process in 'laying in' the early stages of a painting. The other being a brilliant sculptor also

> gave a working demo culminating in a fabulous polar bear which he donated to auction for charity. I had no such bells and whistles but gave a talk for budding Creatives. Although petrified of public speaking, if you speak about something that means so much to you the nerves tend to take a hike – it's more like chatting and sharing what you would love them to know about what you do, if they are interested to hear it. (Writer Viv Groskop is a brilliant help on all things stage fright if needed.) This was a really lovely engagement of a different vibe – if you've anything left in the voice or the tank after prepping and opening, consider this.

Having your own show is a fantastic step to start your career. What you don't sell will find its way in time to its forever home, or could, if there's enough, become a stand-alone collection that a gallery would like to show (ask along everyone you want to work with!). Having stock is a very good thing – you're ready to be discovered and you're ready to go.

And You: Firstly, you are your own best ambassador – when people invest in your work they are investing in you. So while you may need to work away tucked in your turret, you must get out there and meet actual people who might like what you do too.

Secondly, it is good to be part of a creative network that might suit your vibe. It can be a real boost when you are feeling stuck, stagnant or struggling in your flow. You make contacts and have a sense of connection – take a little time for this. It might be a formal network like the Creative Entrepreneurs (I'm a fan of business courses they run in the UK). Similarly, The Dots – join them. They're the LinkedIn for Creatives. The Biscuit Factory is a fabulously supportive business scene for Irish Creatives – Tara Prendergast is a very real artist's ally. These are just a few – you might prefer others – but the point is to connect with others who have commercial skills to teach you. Less formally, there are some great Facebook communities for Creatives, where contacts are shared and comradery is offered. Double treat.

Thirdly, if you find yourself a bit lonesome in your solitary workspace you might want to consider again shared or purpose-built studios where you can chat over the canvas shredder. For less messy types, community workspace enterprises like Second Home (there are others) are wonderful as a physical social network. These are a great option for those who want to work alone at a desk, but in an entrepreneurial community, in a downtown funky setting with pretzels, a brew and a view.

If getting out there and amongst it isn't what you feel like, remind yourself of the importance of at least having connections in support of your art. Most valuable of all is having a little group of contemporaries who you can toss concerns and ideas around with, who you can laugh with and cry with and generally work out how to make the most out of this crazy road trip going forward, together.

Be in Touch

No Creative is an island – thankfully.

To connect

Creative Entrepreneurs, UK – www.creativentrepreneurs.co
(no it doesn't have a .uk)

The Dots, UK – www.the-dots.com

The Biscuit Factory, Ireland – www.thebiscuitfactory.ie
(join Tara's FB group Bite the Biscuit too)

To stay savvy

Artquest in the UK – www.artquest.org.uk

Visual Artists Ireland – www.visualartists.ie

Writers & Artists – www.writersandartists.co.uk

To stay solvent

HMRC – www.gov.uk

Taxaid – www.taxaid.com

The Irish Revenue – www.revenue.ie

Grants and Bursaries for Creatives – investigate 'savvy' websites above, also:

Arts Council UK – www.artscouncil.org.uk

Arts Council Ireland – www.artscouncil.ie

Artist's resale rights, copyright licensing, royalties and payback:

DACS – www.dacs.org.uk

Ivaro – www.ivaro.ie

General IP info:

The Intellectual Property Office UK – www.ipo.gov.uk

The Intellectual Property Office Ireland – www.ipoi.gov.ie

To explore

Creative residencies – pick up your atlas!

Young Creatives, Creatives in a rut, Creatives seeking horizons new – Artist-in-residence programmes are a fabulous way to get outside your usual rhythms – go live, work and explore somewhere inspiring. Search the opportunities on the websites listed above to begin. If you can't find the exact fit, why not contact your dream residency asking if they have considered such a thing and what you could offer them in return? #don'taskdon'tget.

Be a little bold. Be organised, be informed, be confident, be curious, be your own work's greatest supporter. Now go on – get yourself out there.

SECTION VII: FRONT COVER

So how exactly is your introduction to the big world yonder going to go?!

If the very idea of PR and marketing fills you with horror, that sounds just about right. Self-promotion is anathema to many of us Creatives who are often introverted bunnies. The rub is this – we hate to (a) show off or (b) be intrusive, but we need to get our work seen by people who would like to see it. Misjudging the balance can see us tipping over from showing up on relevant radars (necessary) to being a pest (nightmare). Work this out early. You need to do your creativity justice but just do it in a discerning, well-thought-out fashion, with panache.

PR is more organic than advertising, less hard sell, and is generally free if you do it yourself. Although it's just one wand in your marketing wizardry, we will spend some time on it here. You and your creativity are intrinsically linked – intimately so and everything you ever do out there in the public eye becomes part of your art's PR.

I'm not saying marketing is only about PR – there are other matters to consider – but the focus of **Chapter 18** will be on it. Afterwards, **Chapter 19** delves (not too vastly) into the (very vastly) world of the internet, and how to make the most of it for Getting Your Art Out There. You don't need to embrace all of it (you absolutely need time to create) but a little digital razzle dazzle might do wonders for your work.

The beauty of art is engagement – well we'd better get on and engage.

Chapter 18

HELLO WORLD

'We ask ourselves, 'Who am I to be brilliant, gorgeous, talented, fabulous?' Actually, who are you not to be? ... Your playing small does not serve the world.... We are all meant to shine, as children do.'

— Marianne Williamson —
Author and Spiritual Lecturer

I want you have a handle on how this marketing malarky all works. I know that the idea of selling yourself (figuratively!) can be hard – but when you find your work in the Sunday Times *Culture* magazine or on the front cover of the FT's *How To Spend It* you'll be glad you took a deep breath, got plucky and did it.

Done properly, your PR is not nebulous hype, nor is it intrusive – it is a fabulous tool to connect what you do with people who want what you have to offer. If you see it this way the very concept won't leave you in dread – it will excite you instead. It is about putting your creativity in front of an audience that is interested in it, and getting to grips with it will be totally worth your while.

With every PR interaction, you are building trust in your art and in the you behind your art. It may be a very gradual movement of engagement. Done well, your PR shouldn't be uncomfortable; on the contrary, it is about building relationships, not forcing them.

Fledgling PR

Ideally, this should be something you start thinking about as soon as you decide you want your art to be Known. Begin thinking early days about how you might raise your profile and gain industry recognition. Search online for what might be happening in your field; some of the websites mentioned in the last chapter are good starting points. Remember those competitions and award schemes – get amongst them. You might think of writing articles in your area of specialism – this isn't just for writers. Isn't a young fashion designer the best person to write up on young fashion? A mime artist to spill the best beans on mime? Write about your personal take on your subject to connect and think topically. For example, how can resourceful Creatives ride current changing tides? What is your unique experience and how could that help others? Include images and links to your work – be a voice, be a guide, be creative.

Building PR

Your PR isn't only about getting publicity for a specific gig. You want to become – and stay – relevant, and the best way to do this is to remind your audience from time to time that you're still here (Hello…?). One very obvious option is to employ PR experts but this won't always be financially feasible. Also, our shows/works/exhibitions might not feel 'big' enough to bring in the Big Guns. These days there's no reason why you can't be your own PR guru. It's simply a matter of making lots and lots of lists and even more importantly, casting your vision OUT THERE. Starting here:

Your Ideal Audience: First things first. Who are they and where are they? As your art develops and broadens, so will your audience. Keep on top of this – pitch to an evolving public. Whereas once you might have been grateful for the attention of students, these students will, inevitably, age. Remember to target them in their new iteration, as well as their student replacements. Audiences are just people, and people evolve, grow up, progress. Who do you see your work connecting with? What are they reading? And listening to? What digital platforms are they on? To stay relevant you have to stay one step ahead.

Your Ideal Coverage: Where do you want to be featured? Your ideal audience above will dictate your starting points – thereafter – be willing to aim high. Why not? A spread in *Rolling Stone Magazine*? It might feel unattainable – but it's only unattainable *right now*. Think of the journey – you have your destination, now set your course. Leaping to *Rolling Stone* is probably a bit too far a jump at the moment, so you need to put some stepping stones in place. Start with one nearest to you. What is attainable? A local paper? The magazine where your ex-flatmate is working as a receptionist? Acorns to oak trees, remember.

Event PR

At certain points in your upward trajectory you will need to get more proactively PR prepped, particularly in the lead up to a launch event.

Your Campaign: Start early to build a list of niche slots and columns you can pitch for. Check out any press on your peers who are doing well – have a look at the press section on their websites and coverage they shared on social media. Where are they being featured? Might these journalists be interested in what you are doing when it comes to your noteworthy event? It makes sense to get familiar with journalists interested in your sector whose style impressed and whose subject matter resonated.

Approaching the Media: It won't be broadcast news that you are a Creative (although of course I would celebrate this on a plinth at every turn). Use the focal point of a major event but, unless you are already a big name, this in itself won't be enough. It must appeal in terms of something that will turn their readers heads. In order to get PR coverage they must see something of interest to the audience they write for and that makes them want to cover it.

Can you think of what might make a good feature piece? A different angle, some current affairs to hang the piece on? How is what you are doing relevant in the context of these times and trends? What is it about what you do or your journey to doing it that is that bit different to your contemporaries (remember that 'special something')? Spell out what you are doing that sets you that bit apart. Or think about a 'day in the life' column? Great to show a more 3D version of you.

Thereafter, three cardinal rules:

Get it to the right person.
Get it to them in a way that works for them.
Get it in on time.

Where to Send: Pick your ideal (and suitable) publications. Then pick up a copy (if they run a hard copy) of those you are approaching and submit your information in a way that you could see appealing and fitting with their style and formatting. Think beyond the written word to podcasting, radio coverage and their social media postings too. You want to offer something you genuinely think could merrily fill some column inches or airtime or at least click with their regular brief. Begin by checking contact information on the website or, if a printed publication, details will be near the front. I like to telephone the switchboards of hard-copy publications to find out who best to email, double-checking email details. It's great to get a voice who might tell you that the features section is full but perhaps the diary column could give you a chirpy call-out instead.

These days those who will write about you tend to be accessible directly through Twitter and Instagram and other social media. Many give website or email links and detail how they like to be contacted. Follow and engage (authentically) when it feels right, and appropriate. For goodness sake, don't stalk or make them want to block you. Remember – panache…

How to Send: Think beyond just sending your details to someone who might be able to help; that's akin to sending them a note saying 'Here's some work for you to do'. Do as much as you can from the outset to make the proposal more attractive. Unless a journalist specifies otherwise, I suggest a press release by email:

- **The press release**: A press release is a must in my book if you wish to alert your audience (even if it's just an audience of one) to a forthcoming event or a specific piece of work. Some consider it 'old school', but it is an efficient and effective way to summarise exactly what you wish to convey. Put careful thought into it – straightforward and honest connection – you only get one bite. Use a 12 point standard font (Arial/Times New Roman – no jazz hands) with double line spacing for clear presentation. This is how it should go:

  - A good headline to catch interest and explain what the press release is about – you want them to want to read on.
  - Time, date and venue for your 'event'.
  - Get your newsworthy content in here in one line.
  - Get in your USP and get in what is interesting about what you are doing.

- More information (in decreasing level of importance but still aim to intrigue!) that will help write an accurate piece.
- A short overview of who you are as a Creative.
- Contact details and social media links.

If you're unsure, do a quick online search and take a peek at standard formats. Or ask Creative friends for examples of theirs. And get a friend to cast an eye – sometimes we miss the most obvious points – they might be to us too obvious to think to include. Think about that 'hook' – that reason the journalist will be glad you got in touch. It will get you from deleted to delighted – find it!

- **The email**: Having crafted a cracker full of enticing information, don't just fire it out there. Each approach must be considered, concise and tailored to the journalist you are writing to.
  - Address them by name and be aware of their typical column/feature/contribution, in terms of structure/format/style/tone. They may have specific requests around this in their bios – follow them if so.
  - Outline why you believe they and you to be a good fit – convey why you think what you are doing might be relevant and of interest to them. Bespoke, not blunderbuss please.
  - Include a low-res jpeg in the body of the email. Don't send attachments – you can forward high res on request. (For print magazines and any publications of the visual arts a really good image can bring it to life for them and swing it for you.)

- Cut and paste the text of the press release into a clearly separated section below your introductory paragraph.
- If they have specified that they don't require a press release, make sure instead that your tailored synopsis is on the money with all relevant details and include your contact details and social media links to sign off.
- Offer to forward a detailed bio if required.

Make it easy for them – a pleasure even! Bear in mind that journalists get dozens, sometimes hundreds of cold-call emails a day. You have about five seconds to make an impression. Don't lose them on the subject line – tailor it so they open with anticipation not ennui. Try to give them something different from every other event they are pursued to cover so that it will be a joy for them to include. Be nice, spellcheck, be grateful and, again, be a little bit bold.

When to Send: If you're publicising an event, make a backwards schedule of lead times for all your media contact list. Diarise who needs to receive what when, and everything that you need to action right up to the day before launch. Find out the lead times required – it varies from a week (online updates) and two to three weeks (for local hard copy media) to six months (the glossies), depending on the publications. To be included in all the 'what's on' listings: Google 'submit an event listing' + your geographical area of focus, at least 14 days before.

Send your emails mid-week between 10 a.m. and 2 p.m. – this is their less frantic time. You can follow up after a few days to see if they received it if you haven't heard back – politely and appreciative of how inundated they may be. Make sure you have everything in place when you hit the button on your PR – updated bios, websites, further images, stylist for your live interview (!) etc. You need to be ready to engage.

Some Notes to Note: I am not saying any of this will guarantee coverage – column inches are precious and can be hard won. But it is certainly possible. It needs to be done properly, but the results might just see you chuffed. At the very least you will have honed your own story and key messages for your social media campaign, which is absolutely key in your marketing and one definitely best handled by you.

If instead you choose to employ a freelance PR professional, make sure it is someone who is familiar with your world and has the contacts in your field, and who properly interprets what you and your work are about. It needs to be worth your budget. Always sign off on what is going out. One wrong word/nuance has made me feel nauseous; the tone of the article is so important – this is your chance to convey exactly what you are doing, this is about YOU.

Non-PR Marketing Options

PR has its place – especially when you have something specific to tell the world (apart from "I'm HERE!"). But Marketing should be a constant beat in your creative song. Sometimes you turn it up, sometimes it fades into the background – but you always have it as a background hum.

Your Other Marketing Moves

- **Get your art online**: Obviously. So obviously, in fact, that the next chapter deals exclusively with this.
- **Get connecting**: The word 'networking' to me is unattractive. We don't want to 'catch' people, we want to connect with them instead.

Connecting is the greatest form of marketing. Others get to know you and your art; you get to know others who – well you never know where things will lead! This is what you need to tell yourself when you would rather stick pins in your eyes than go to an industry event/an art exhibition/a dance recital. Of course, if you're delighted to go to an event, don't bluster in expecting to fill your Little Black Book; go hoping to have a nice time and see or learn something new, and if you meet new people – how wonderful.

Formal gatherings aren't the only way to make connections of course. A really nice connectivity method is to get involved in your community: donate artwork for local charities or auctions, go talk to the children in your local school, run a local competition … It's marketing, it's connecting, and it's community-building-wonderful.

- **Get dramatic**!: How much TV do you watch? Next time you're staring at the box, look at the spaces and walls behind the actors. Some backdrops aren't organised, but most – especially in interior shots – very much are. Do you see paintings? Sculpture? Is a dance studio featured? Do the fictional characters have logos they use? Is that something you could provide? Don't assume that television and streaming shows are all produced by flash organisations with millions to spend – not at all. Most are produced by hard-working Creatives, working for small production companies, who might be delighted to get an out-of-the-blue call from an artist offering a solution to their blank backdrops. Get searching online, and asking around.

- **Get funded**: Apart from the very obvious benefits to getting some additional funding for your art, there are marketing benefits too. Art grants are often accompanied by media coverage, and always accompanied in the art world by some level of kudos. Having a funding award on your creative CV reads great. So keep your eyes and ears open. It's worth really putting the effort in to these applications, and again, get a new set of eyes on them before you press send.

Anything and everything can be marketing. Think beyond the obvious. Work with what you have – your medium, your location, your finances, your connections – and think creatively about getting into the public eye. Get going now – growing an audience as you are growing into your bigger creative shoes can only be a good thing. Cast a stone outside your studio four walls. Watch the ripples spread.

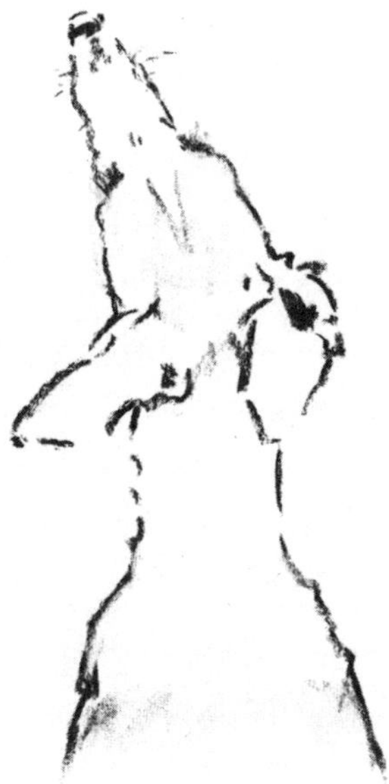

Chapter 19

INTO THE ETHER

'I want to put a ding in the Universe'

— Steve Jobs —

The internet isn't just for distractions, lovely Creatives (although I know too what bliss in that direction lies). Tucked within its layers are myriad marketing opportunities winking at us daily should we be at the point when we wish to share our work with the wider world. Granted you need to focus on the job in hand and pick your platforms in these times where folk appear to feel that no aspect of their lives is un-fascinating, but it's the easiest tool for getting your valid and worthy work out there. (As soon as I type '*The End*', 'poof!' a new cyber showroom never even dreamt of will be born, so I write this chapter in a whisper.)

A knock-on effect of the pandemic has been that digital sharing has manifested itself as mainstream in the arts. It will never be a substitute for 'up close and personal' and really breathing it in, but what a welcome addition when we can't get to the ballet ourselves. We will continue to rush through the turnstiles at any opportunity, but streaming a live opera/exhibition/book reading into our sitting rooms is a glorious phenomenon too. In this way, we are extremely lucky – we can be 'out there' while being tucked up and cosy 'in here'. Hip and hygge (if slightly demented) together.

If you are tipping from pastime to pro and creating for commercial ends you need to get to grips with marketing through the internet to promote what you do. Here's why:

Collections: Auction houses, galleries, dealers and agents are all using digital media to speak directly to their audiences, so you really should too. Some of the biggest collectors in the world are buying their visual art online – it is worth making yourself visible so you may just be spotted. Record labels and publishing houses are finding their 'next big thing' in musicians and writers who have already self-published in the online space. Ed Sheeran and EL James were just two. Creatives are no longer going mainstream through the traditional channels; sometimes they won't even need them. Artists of all art forms, you can upload your work and instantly reach your following: a potential global audience, or that lucky break, a finger click away. Excited yet?!

Connections: I believe that it helps us when we have connection with like-minded Creatives, for the sake of our sanity and of our art. Think of the role the Parisian café scene played in the culturally ground-breaking emergence of the movement of modern art. Ditto the Glasgow Boys coming together and the Bloomsbury Set ruffling artistic feathers. Creativity doesn't grow in a vacuum. Pooling and sharing, mutual encouragement and support, cross-pollination of influences and ideas all provide the backdrop for great creative advancement. As I've already said – and you already know – we need solitude, but we also need connection to thrive. In our multi-dutied and heavily-committed lives we may not be able to share exchanges together over *un café* in Montmartre, but we can take advantage of the virtual interaction opportunities we have.

Indeed in this digital era, co-creation and collaboration become possible through connections that otherwise would never be made.

Everyone you need to connect with from a business perspective has a social media pulse. Tap in. And yes, it's an ever-evolving and daunting world out there but it's also still full of ordinary human beings like you and me, in search of art and beauty and music and musings and all things 'meaning of life'.

Distractions: (Yes these can be a good thing – there is life beyond your own creative perch.) Even if you are just enjoying your creativity for yourself you might like to share insights and outcomes with a wider audience than the robins outside your studio. The feedback can be useful, and heartwarming, and on down days – when the creative juices aren't so much flowing as stagnating – playing about with your chosen platform, updating your profile, adding new colour schemes, checking out the new creative kid in town, *whatever,* can be a happy and productive use of time.

These are just some of the reasons I want you to harness the power of the World Wide Web, in your pyjamas, from your kitchen. And here's how:

Your Social Media

Getting to grips with social media means you can be your own marketing main man – which makes financial, as well as authentic, sense. Unless you have a superb gallery/recording studio/publishing house and an established reputation behind you (and even then), it's a really important tool to use in selling your work.

If you are serious about sharing your creativity with those whom it might just touch, you need to develop and manage your social media presence in a way that is true to you. You can pop up on the radar of people who need to find you, and you them, once you learn to use it in a way that serves you. It's the ultimate Creatives' launch room (and water cooler, as you wish) in the cloud.

What I have learned so far:

1. For visual artists, I can't stress enough the importance of uploading your images *somewhere*. Like it or loathe it, get on it. Instagram is the visual Creatives' platform of choice – it's friendly, supportive and generally troll-free. I would caution frugality on Facebook (unless you have a business page); overloading personal relationships with our work can come across as a bit showy-offy. A little less can sometimes be so very much more (channel your Coco Chanel), plus we hate to bore. Facebook is however good for spreading the word. Do use it, and all social outlets, as a signpost to your work/publication/showtime as and when you need to. You might also consider setting up a separate page dedicated to your work, in which case post to your heart's content. Pinterest hasn't transpired to be the selling platform intended but it's great to create mood boards for inspiration and as a global gallery for your visual work to be seen. Twitter unnerved me when old What'shisname hijacked it, but I know it's an effective support community, particularly for those whose metier is the written word. I enjoy connecting in there but it's good to know where the mute button is. TikTok is also fun and brings its own up-vibe to the party. It has a much more playful feel – less posey and trolly more general rocking out – and a wide audience that otherwise might miss you. It is a no-brainer for those in the performing arts but I know artists like me who are using it too, and loving it, sharing and collaborating – think theatrics, great music backdropping your work, time-lapse videos, collaboration opportunities and sharing what you do with humour and fun. I will if you will.

2. You don't need to be on all of them; it's better to do one or two really well. You'll know what feels right for you, your work and your time constraints. My comfort zone is Instagram and I know writers and musicians who love the supportive vibe in there too. It is a good gallery wall for the visual arts but video allows for sharing of performances and there is plenty of room for catchy written content too. Where Twitter is a rave, circa 1996, Instagram is a feel-good well-mannered cocktail party – if you make an effort people are generally really nice, interested and polite. It feels like healthy engagement, not too intrusive and you can gently move on if they become weird. Your Facebook posts are more easily shared by others, so perhaps mix it up between the two.

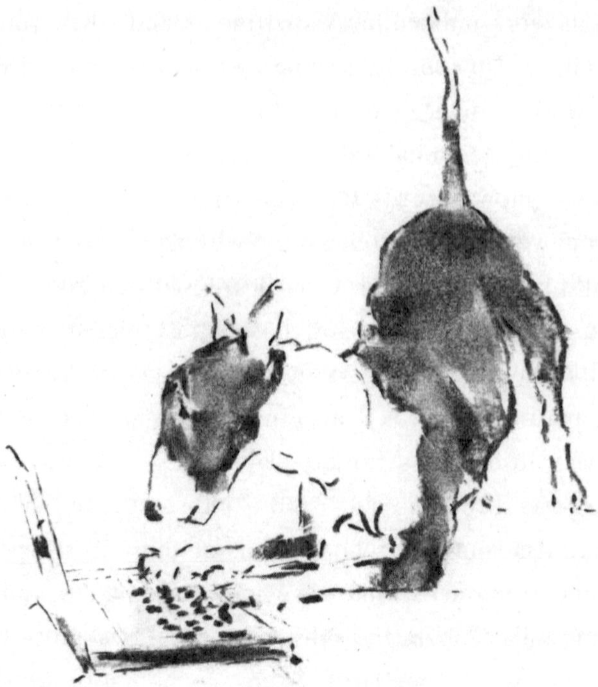

3. Set up your profiles with bios that accurately describe who you are and which are relevant to the work you wish to share and audience you wish to attract. It's a very small window of attention you get – don't leave them guessing. Include your website address in there too. (You *do* have a website, don't you?)

4. Once set up you need people to follow you, share you, like what you do and interact with you. Get your pals onboard, your grandmother, the postman. Momentum breeds momentum and we all need a leg-up to begin. (To make this more appealing make sure you put up good content in the first place that people are in fact happy to share. Without good content the initial sparks won't ignite.)

5. Use Hashtags. I don't need to tell you that, do I? Hashtags ('#' – think librarian cataloguing) get you found by people who need to find you. Hashtags are essentially flags by which your audience might find you and your work. Get to understand them, then use them. Use lots of them to begin with. Also use them straight away. Added in as an afterthought in a caption or edit may mean you have missed the target audience window – things move quickly out there. Using hashtags as markers for your work will ultimately help you build your brand if that is what you are seeking to do.

6. Use videos. Video views are exploding across all digital media – it is the way forward to increase engagement on your social channels and to showcase what you do. Videos really focus on who you are behind the work, and this can be key, especially where interaction in real life is limited. Let your personality come through

and show them the Creative they can connect with. You want to share not just finished creative work but glimpses into the back-drop – your processes, your inspirations, all that goes into making your work what it ultimately is – bring your audience with you. Video is super supportive of this. YouTube (if you have a channel) can be used for longer recordings but Facebook and Instagram are brilliant for soundbites and snippets and demos 'on the fly'.

The great thing is that once made, you can use the same video across all your media and it is so easily shareable by others when appealing to those who might share it. And you don't need to be an ultra pro – your phone is grand to use and totally relatable (unless your creative expertise is in a field that can do better!). Choose landscape mode for recording for YouTube, website and email send-outs, while portrait is better for Instagram and Facebook stories. Press record – keep yourself in shot – don't decapitate like half our childhood photos of gap-toothed us on our batty pony. Get it in the can without too much repetition or swearing, free-styling is great but remember why you are recording.

7. In all your online media use titles, tags and captions creatively and well – this is an opportunity for you to build a presence that people will connect with. Try to keep a consistent tone, style and message content across the different platforms you decide to use – this is your brand so stay with the palette that reflects it and you.

8. Ideally share consistently too in terms of when you post – just as in real-life relationships, you need to make the effort to keep in touch. Quite nice to throw in a picture that includes your good self (apparently one in every nine posts should comprise YOU) – again – great to remind folk you're not a faceless business and you really exist.

9. Keep your professional hat on for the sake of your work – first impressions are powerful. And have your hand on the handbrake for anything that might compromise your vision for your creativity. Once out there it will be digitally independent, doing its own thing.

10. It is important to step up to the stage with the right mindset. Before publishing content think 'share' and 'connect', *never* hard sell. It's sometimes worth a short conversation with self – am I sharing in a good way or am I just being a peacock? Be cool. And keep your sense of humour.

11. Share others' work in your posts – it's supportive and it's nice, and the universe will always listen and reciprocate. My social media pet hate: people who follow you for you to follow back, and then – unfollow you – seriously?

12. Always be kind.

Work your Website

Every artist needs at least a one-page point of reference with a professional looking image, your own domain name and an email address. But please give us more. These days constructing a simple website couldn't be easier. The more tech-savvy amongst you will want to build more expansively which is great, better and better. We are reassured, when investing in the arts, when we can do a quick search to see who each other is, if we're still alive and creating, and generally what we're all about …

For those of you selling your creative wares or hoping to be commissioned for work in your specialised field, a website is imperative. There are some excellent and totally manageable DIY platforms to choose from, which require no knowledge of computer language or HTML – Squarespace and Wix are two of the most popular. If you are thinking of expanding your audience via a blog, consider one of these platforms as they incorporate this facility. For what it's worth, my own experience with Squarespace has been a joy – real people answer my every question (in relation to my website in any case!). They have beautifully designed easy-to-use templates (I use Avenue) all up and running and ready to rock. All have a sophisticated clean line minimalistic vibe, which I love – as do my paintings. And then there's the integrated e-commerce system that even I could manage. And if you're just dipping your toe in the water it lets you start with a simple cover page and you can build it when you're ready from there. It works for me.

When selecting and registering your website name choose a reputable domain name registrar. Hop online and find one that's popular or ask your techy buddies – I am reluctant to recommend specific businesses as it's such a fast-changing industry, however I have used www.godaddy.com and www.blacknight.com and found both to be great. Brainstorm your ideal site names (the wholly ideal one of course being your own name as an artist), aim for the .com version but don't let it throw you completely if you can't acquire it. If registering .com try to buy up the related suffixes too, especially for the jurisdictions or practice areas relevant to you (e.g. co.uk/.ie/.us or .net/.org). It's not expensive and will help strengthen your brand down the line. Check that the name you go for is not already being used as a business name or limited company in your geographical territory.

Whichever platform you choose remember, of course, to make it mobile friendly (opt for a 'responsive' theme) and try to use lots of images – visuals are key and again videos rock. Include working links to your social media accounts and you might even spend a winter's day attempting to understand SEO.

Uhoh, SEO?: *Search Engine Optimisation.* In simple terms you want to use words (keywords) that people would use to search for content like yours. When they search on the great big web you want to appear somewhere where they can find you, so the higher up you sit in Google 'rankings' the better. To do this the words they look up in Google need to be reflected in the keywords you use throughout your website. With this in mind use words specific to your niche but do include more generic terms too. Videos are ace for SEO (Google owns YouTube so using videos where you can has become important in upping your rankings). Algorithms love them and linked properly they will have you leaping up the page. Other actions that will have you leaping are website updates, media mentions and regular blog posting (when writing either blog or newsletter content – link back to your own website pages where you can). These all send signals to Google's radar field that you are up and at it and active and so help boost your SEO.

As do 'reciprocal links'. These are links to your website or blog from others, and reciprocated vice versa, valuable especially if they have a strong presence in your field. Including them also demonstrates industry interaction and respect – so again you want to write good content that they want to share. SEO aside, cross support is always a confidence boost. If this is all a cyberstep too far, get some help with it – there are excellent small business tech folk out there who speak SEO and all things digital fluently – call one.

Finally for your website – include any press coverage and testimonials if relevant (and good!). People feel better about investing in you when they see that your work is been appreciated by others. In this vein, include your accolades from competitions and awards – I always curtsy even deeper to my contemporaries when this reads well. Be sure to include a 'subscribe' button on your landing pages so that people can 'opt in' to your growing mailing list – you'd hate them to miss out.

Nail the Email

Next up – your email list which is, since Chapter 17, organised. It is a marketing marvel, at the end of your fingertips, and algorithm free (no smoke and mirror shenanigans – you send, it arrives, hooray).

As previously mentioned, your list and practices need to be GDPR compliant. You can tie in your first mail-out of your creative news with a friendly GDPR compliant hello to make sure you are remaining (a) legal and (b) relevant. Both are key. You need to figure who is in and who is out. Make this first mail out so appealing that they will want to stick around but totally respect if they don't – your electrician may not be interested in hearing about your brilliant brushstrokes or blockbuster ideas – his loss.

You will use your email list for direct comms and invitations of course, but in between champagne events you need to keep some momentum. It is worth getting your head around an email marketing platform like Mailchimp if you're planning on going big (hint – you are …). It will keep you efficient and informed and looking like a bit of a pro. In using an emailing marketing system you can track and see how your send-out is doing. The click and open data will tell you (the unsubscribes will tell you too, but not to dwell). It also helps you categorise your recipients into different groups and you can use this for more tailored marketing. I got in a bit of a muddle harvesting the addresses from email opt-ins by an unconnected link back to my website so do a quick practice run on your nearest and dearest before hitting the button for real.

Once your email list is up to date and email management system honed there are a few more marketing moves you might consider. These are my suggested digital pigeons to carry your messages beyond your studio walls:

The Newsletter

Starting a newsletter is a good way to make deeper connections and stronger relationships with people who have subscribed to you already. And its reach needn't grind to a halt with your already listening listeners. You can gather new interest sharing a nicely designed bulletin through your social media too.

Interesting info and updates aside, it lands via your mailing list to remind people that you're doing your thing for when your thing is called for. This is good. Also good is using it as a way to make some income between 'the big nights out'. You can share work you've just finished in a 'this is what I've been up to' way. Or introduce a studio sale or silent auction – great to find homes for those pieces that have been keeping you company when it's time to make room for more.

Some tips for your nicely designed newsletter:

- Keep it simple, to the point and catchy. A good title with a short intro followed by your various news bites.

- *Obviously* announce upcoming events/performances/shows (they get top billing) but include anything of newsworthy note – any wins or whims pertaining to your current creative career.

- Consider your aesthetic content – take the opportunity to showcase what you do. Pro shots are fab but happy snaps from behind the scenes can be really relatable and interesting – mixing it up is good.

- Include links to anything you wish them/they might like to engage with – a blog, a podcast, an e-book, a YouTube video clip.

- Link in to media mentions (good for SEO and self-esteem). This shouldn't be 'wow go me' but a feel-good share as many of your email subscribers will already have supported you and it's in the interests of their investment that they know you are doing well.

- The quiet moments can be of interest too to those curious about the creative work you do. A look behind your studio curtain to your processes etc. can be lovely.

- Have you any interesting bite-sized insights into relevant industry news? Share them.

- Have you had a recent creative adventure? A residency, a recce, a trip to your inspiration? You might curate a list of creative works that inspire you most, and drip feed these as '*amuses-bouches*' as the issues roll out.

- You might include previews or offers that you wouldn't put into a blog to thank them for being in your team.

- For those who aren't feeling it– you must allow them away with an obvious 'unsubscribe' (working link!) button, although of course you'd be sad to see them go. You want everyone to choose your comms, not endure them.

Many believe that the efficient newsletter supersedes the more wordy blog but I disagree. Both are valuable marketing tools and both have their place. Pandemic pottering saw many of us take more time to engage in worthy endeavours (reading! The Arts!) where previously such opportunities were lost in our hyper state of life on-the-go. I appreciate the soundbites of a newsletter but I know that I love a juicy blog by favoured writers landing in for my morning biscuit break.

The Blog

The blog post is the more journalistic, curious and focused younger sibling of the newsletter. A more intense little sister. If that sounds onerous (and a bit scary), it's not: it's opportunity. Subjects you might touch on in a newsletter can be expanded upon and explored more deeply in here. More 'macro' in focus than 'this is what I am up to right now'. You can use it to ripple out what you know to those who don't yet know you. Think entertaining, inspirational or even educational writings on themes relating to your creative work.

Beginning your Blog:

- Think about focusing the lens further behind the scenes in your creative life. You might want to show more of yourself behind the work that you do. This warm hello-step-inside-my-art-nest vibe is relatable and engaging and can help build an emotional connection with those that begin to engage.
- Or go more high-brow – is there an angle of your industry you have a distinct opinion on or expertise in? Have you something you can give interesting commentary on, or good advice about, that others might like to read about? Become an industry name. Writing 'relevant' content garners credence in your authority in your creative field. (Also valuable should you wish to teach in your discipline later down the line).
- To mix it up you might want to highlight others who inspire and contribute in the industry, and to celebrate others' creative works which you know your audience would appreciate too. There may be interesting people you would like to interview? Remember

those sparking collaborations? (This might inspire an inspiring podcast too?!)

- Guest blogging (writing content for another industry-linked blog or having a guest on yours) will see you sharing valuable new (interested) audiences, and including reciprocal links between you helps everyone's SEO. Way to go.

Your Platform: There are various blog platforms to choose from – investigate which one is right for you. Some of my wordsmith friends use (and love) Wordpress and whilst there will be a bit of a learning curve involved it allows for detailed customisation, stars in SEO and gets rave reviews all round. Wix and Squarespace both get great thumbs up too and might be easier for you to use. There are of course others that might suit your creative requirements better but just make sure you choose one which won't overawe or fill you with tech-dread each time you set to it. Avoid those that require coding skills unless you're a coder or plan to start dating one soon.

Your Plan: Plot a series of posts before you launch – at least three to four – as you want your themes to flow. Decide how often to publish – quarterly/monthly /weekly/daily (do you never sleep?!) depending how inspired or interesting you are likely to feel (again know thyself, and thine commitments). Be realistic, no one will judge you for not posting on a loop – just aim to be consistent. And quality is king.

Aim too for consistency in font, format and (roughly) length. In terms of format – simple works. You can go all out but if an image on a plain white wall is good enough for Saatchi it's good enough for me. Also in terms of instant appeal, not only will your blog need a clever name, each post should ideally be enticingly titled to draw the on-the-fencers in.

Helpfully, your platform will archive your posts chronologically so that when your writings come up on someone's radar they have easy access to more. This finding and re-finding system means that once posted, your blogs are accessible and shareable thereafter. Always include links for your readers to share through social media and via email and an email 'opt-in' to grow that precious mailing list consistently.

Behind your blog you have your 'Stats' – the statistics of who has read what, when, which country they were in, how many times a post has been read etc. (Good for the feedback loop but I'm reliably informed by some well-known blogger friends that these stats can become all engrossing. You have been warned.)

So Which Pigeon?: Newsletters are mighty efficient and have a high return on send-out ratio due to their already opted-in audience, however, blogs have longer legs and a greater potential wingspan. This is because they are created using tools and systems independent of your email list. They exist in a separate web space, each archived, with their own grown up 'url'. They can be shared independently and can get you out there and build a following with audiences new.

The newsletter performs as a monologue – when sent out you don't really expect a reply. This might suit you when your head is deep in preps and studio work. A blog, on the other hand, can start conversations. The comments people leave are real feedback (not just 'click' styles) – you will know how your content is actually going down and can learn, progress, adapt, develop, hone (all these good words) from there.

It is worth mentioning that many manage to monetise their blogs by including sponsored content or ads of some kind. It just requires that the blog receive a certain number of hits (people reading) per post, or over a specified time (a week or a month are the norm). Newsletters can of course have sponsored content, but generally tend not to. (See links for regulations p.195).

Whichever you go for align your style with your overall brand and *of course* you'll have included linked icons throughout to all your social media too.

So to keep in touch or to spread the word further, or generally to keep 'relevant' (if that's important to you), think how each of these two media modes might work for you. Should you do both you may not have time to actually get on and create anything to write about. However, literary Creatives/those who enjoy the crafting of the written word/those who don't sleep might want to take on the two. Respect.

The Vlog

The (video log) is another sibling – the more extroverted one in the family. I've already sung the benefits of the video; this – as you would gather – is a blog in video format. Your written content is replaced by video content and gives blogger you the chance to go video viral. In a good way.

Obviously a vlog shares content for watchers and listeners instead of readers, and will play to different skillsets and areas of creativity. Some of you will be happier presenting than writing (and of course it lends itself beautifully as a medium to those in the performing arts #shownottell). It might also make an appealing change for many solitary studio bunnies to shake it up and get their warpaint on.

YouTube, which is the main vlogging platform, clocks up over 70,000 video views per second. (Facebook and Instagram are popular too.) All three also have livestreaming features for real-time momentum and interaction through live chat – a thought for your braver days. TikTok's also an option if your vlog posts are short and that's where your audience is at. (NB – our audiences are adapting too – there are plenty of grannies getting down with the kids on TikTok – never assume!)

This is all possible with your camera phone and a dash of sass but if getting serious you may want to invest in more serious audio/visual equipment. You might again be considering income potential with a subscription channel, brand advertising, or sponsorship. (I did say think big didn't I?). Do be aware however, that if you are going to advertise other people's wares or services (blogging or vlogging), that you need to comply with some basic advertising rules and regulations. As more brands look to harness influencer marketing, regulators are looking more closely at advertising practices on social media generally. Good resources for this issue are the Advertising Standards Authority: www.asa.org.uk in the UK and the Advertising Standards Authority for Ireland: www.asai.ie.

Hitting The Right Notes

Get your work out there when you're ready – blog/vlog/do virtual acrobats. But with one heck of a caveat – only send out work you're proud of. Once on the internet your work takes on a virtual life of its own. Videos and images will be shared across many platforms when published through social media or your website and they'll forever haunt you if you haven't been your own dragon at your door. Remember when posting that a few good images – even two or three to begin with – are so much more valuable than posting even one lesser representation which will bring the average of your quality down. I don't want to rain on your creative parade – I just really want for you and your work to shine. Now step up to the mic and go.

Conclusion: At the time of writing this I am in my late 40s. When I started eons ago working in the city I used to fire up the big block of technology on the library desk as early as I could muster each morning, before the search engines became painfully slow when America woke up and got 'on the line'. In terms of tech generations, I am practically extinct. But here we now have access to incredible network systems and a way to get our work launched – frugally and instantly – so take the time and effort to up your online game. It can be amazing. I love my analogue pleasures of paper and pens and books, and candlelight not blue lights, but we have to kick off our comfort blankets for the sake of our work sometimes. If this digital dinosaur can, well you can too. Roger that?

And over and out.

SECTION VIII: NOW YOU'RE COVERED!

Lovely Creatives, we've made it. I feel like casting the rucksack aside – arms to the sky and taking a dive bomb into the blue waters of a lagoon. Drink it in. You are courageous, tenacious, and poised for your full potential.

Take a heck of a bow, and keep going.

When we have found ourselves on the backfoot, we have had to steady up and get that front foot forward again. And look how we are rewarded when we do. The keys lie in dedication to your practice, in maintaining your momentum, and developing your resilience at every turn.

On this road we must also be here for our soul buddies. Interaction and connection are where the party's at. So now gather that momentum – you have all the firepower you need. Go chase those now-tangible dreams. And on your way be sure to bring others with you. Inspiration is the currency of creativity – now pass it on.

Chapter 20

DREAMCATCHING

'Don't listen to the dream stealers. Follow your dreams and be kind to others along the way.'

— Bear Grylls —
Adventurer, Writer, Survival Instructor

Dreaming is a serious business. You need to listen in to that inkling that you could attain your 'unattainable' if you dared to imagine yourself at your very best. We are here in this life to rock it out to our maximum potential – so put this on your roaring fire and stoke it.

Be honest with yourself about what your dreams could be, and then invest yourself in a path towards them. Keep building towards the call that is your divine vision and voice. If a little personal anarchy is called for, tap into the rebel you. Many consider the notion of 'following our dreams' to be a selfish indulgence but if circumstances are favourable, remember what happens to the boats on a rising tide! And you are generally in a better position to keep others buoyed up when you are living a life true to you.

Your Vision

You must always think BIG. Try to see beyond the laundry pile and develop a higher vision for your life. Think potential and positivity – set out with a purpose (a steam-iron!) and a dream (crisp linen!). And then a plan. Vision and focus are triggers for their own fulfilment – use them as such. Set your ideal worthy long-range goals that may take years to achieve and start building on your small successes early, i.e. now.

Getting 'there' involves taking your less-than-excellent experiences and mentally rejigging them as good lessons learnt. Cultivate your well-being, each and every day. Build up your life resource account from daily habits towards a strong mental disposition – this is super important for when you need to dip in. Both crikey moments and crisis moments will happen, but you will handle them when they do. Be forgiving to yourself when you hurtle off your path. You can hurtle back on again. Compassion.

Reaching your dreams doesn't come of shortcuts and quick fixes but of a steady build to lift off. It comes of making peace with who you are, how you are, and then deciding where it is you really want to go.

Where did I go? Hard to tell some days! But in the tricky days I still count my blessings for where my creativity has taken me. I think we've settled in nicely together.

From Rags to ... Better Rags!

When I began painting in oils, I decided I would take ten years of practising my art before I would take on any commissions. This thinking was twofold. Firstly – I wanted to be able to do these beautiful animals justice to a meaningful degree, so I set about honing my skills. Secondly, I was determined to be in with a decent shot of fulfilling expectations, if someone was kind enough to invest and trust in me.

I first set out my palette with any serious conviction in 2010, and while painting an early piece on the pavement by Albert Bridge, I sold it for eighty pounds to a passerby. In 2020, a decade to the day, I painted my first private Royal commission.

Other heart-warming moments have made the intervening years' work worthwhile. The loyal pointer who came back home with me from, not one, but two, solo shows, finally, with a flourish, found his way into a book which is now in every major gallery in the world. Neither of us was expecting that. (He was a very special piece to me and I was delighted to take him back home both times – some babies you don't want to let go). Now he sits amongst works by artist heroes – Singer Sargent, Degas, Frink, Freud, Hockney and Nicholson – a long way from the doghouse after all. An anorak alert – I got on the train to Paris just to see the book in the Musee D'Orsay. Getting up at 4.30 am that morning was like Christmas to my creative three-year-old and a firm au revoir to the duvet dragging days gone by.

If it helps at all to share here, I couldn't get a feel of oil paints to save my life when I started. I sat under Albert Bridge and cried. But I also used to go there to daydream. Since then, I have been lucky enough to see a little pattern of dreams that I dared to hold come true. I'm not glossing the glitches – I've had my share of reality checks – but I have had magic moments too. Early on in my daubings, I encountered a kind 'Dragon' who bought some paintings, and this kept me afloat, just when I thought I wouldn't be able to make it work. Thereafter, moments of reward and reassurance have sprung up when needed most, and they tend to arrive in the nick of time. It is always when life feels that bit 'uphill' and a question mark begins to hover over all I set out to do.

My rags have improved dramatically as I continue to work towards my vision and putting my self and my work out there. My hounds' travels keep me both envious and amused... A mini troupe have just cameoed in an acclaimed network drama, and a Baywatch actress in the Hamptons now owns a little happy bull terrier called Pharell. See dreams can be really fun too?! And I promise they offset the bad days, with grace.

I might have had a plan once of a romantic happy ever after. Dolly Alderton's honest writings often tickle me, and recently in her *Sunday Times* agony column she was responding to a young woman's dilemma in the great big choice of her marriage partner. Her advice went as follows: *'Find someone whose company you love, someone who makes you feel alive and safe and understood – those are the specifics you should be looking for; the rest doesn't matter so much.'* It struck me that my art makes me feel that way when we are rocking along nicely together. It has become my partner in so many ways, although like any marriage we have our crashing fallouts too.

For the days that come filled with more doubts than dreams I have to reference the mighty American basketball player, Michael Jordan, here. *'I've missed more than 9,000 shots in my career. I've lost almost 300 games. Twenty-six times, I've been trusted to take the game winning shot and missed. I've failed over and over and over again in my life. And that is why I succeed.'* How many young minds will he have helped with this wise introspection? Good shot.

To be in it for the long game you need to build on your layers of failure, and use them as your fuel. Be focused and be consistent. Be tenacious towards your vision but also be aware of your periphery and for what might come shooting in. Always investigate a twinkling tangent – be open to a plot twist and an even better plan!

Now What??

'Relaxed expectation' – this is the mind frame I would encourage you to have. Notice every step forward as you close the gap between what you want from life and where you started. Take feedback and criticism; thank them for it. Ignore what doesn't serve your higher vision for your work. Map out your vision and lean into your dream with a great BIG FAT YES – attitude *really* matters.

Continue always to develop emotional resilience. Call deep on your courage. Remain ever thankful for your gazillion blessings. Keep learning. Gather the tactics you'll need in your toolkit and use them to do what you want to do with greater understanding. Then go dare to be yourself. Bedazzle, bewilder, and more than anything, believe in yourself and in all you can achieve. And when you are swinging from Jupiter (the planetary giver of gifts and luck) keep humility and compassion to the fore.

Do what you do, intensely, and then let your work speak for itself. See your breakdowns as your awakenings. Flip them – time and time again. Be brave, be stubborn and be bold. All in the service of your own beautiful work. Keep your integrity, and keep your autonomy, and set your compass for your highest self in all you do.

Then down the fireman's pole:

go,

go,

go.

Be brilliant, dear Creative. I dare you.

Chapter 21

PS: PASS IT ON

'Be kind whenever possible. It is always possible.'

— The Dalai Lama —

Someone told me recently that an act of kindness releases a serotonin spike not only in the receiver of that kindness, and the giver, but also in those witnessing the act of kindness taking place. It seems that just observing and being in the energy field of kindness gets the physiological benefits too. Isn't that wonderful?

The sweetness of this science aside, I am always so grateful to the kindness of fellow artists who help, guide and share. Some are so successful you can't believe they would take the trouble, but the artists' community is a field of generous-hearted gems nestling in studios around the globe. I find that when we peek above our parapets, the abundance of altruism and generosity of spirit is life affirming. And if we can help each other, why wouldn't we? Don't let's ever be competitive or envious of our peers' successes. Their win is not my loss – there's enough sunshine for everyone.

In turn, my creative, generous friends, be sure to respond wholeheartedly to those who have turned to you. Altruism fosters a sense of connection, keep the kindness flowing. We are here to increase each other, let's not forget.

'How do we change the world?
One random act of kindness at a time.'

— Morgan Freeman —
Actor, Director & Narrator

Just sayin'.

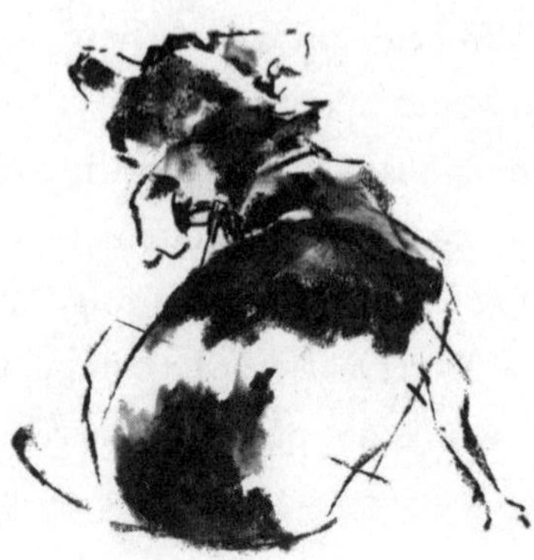

A THANK YOU

I would like to raise a toast to all the great teachers I have found along my creative way.

And to my dear friends who have seen me through the bumpier days. Especially Jess – who got me through my finals in college, a lot of bad dating and the deep end editing process of this book.

Also to Catherine Williams, Melanie Cotton, Jonny Mayner and Nicole Page Croft – talented superstars all.

Finally, to my fabulous and forever supportive family. Angie and Paulo, Siobhan and Jim, Jason, Christy and Hannah – this book is for you too.

Thank you

x

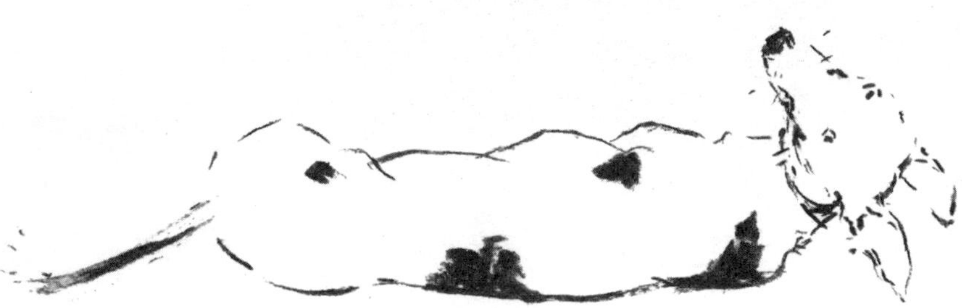

REFERENCE SOURCES

Alderton, Dolly, 'Dear Dolly', *The Sunday Times.*

Barrett, Jamie, 'Failure', '9000 shots', Nike 1997.

Bates, Tony, *Depression: The Common Sense Approach,* 1999, Gill Publishing.

Beck, Martha, *Finding Your Own North Star*, 2001, Piatkus Books, 2001 Crown Publishers of Random House US.

Berkeley University, Dr Matthew Walker, sleep scientist.

Beckett, Samuel, *Worstward H,* 1983, Grove Press.

Caddy, Eileen, *Opening Doors Within,* 2007, Findhorn Press, 1986.

Cameron, Julia, *The Artist's Way,* 1995, Pan, 1994, Souvenir Press Ltd.

Centre For Coaching, International Academy for Professional Development, London.

Charteris, Evan, *John Sargent*, Charles Scribner's Sons, New York, 1927 (referenced by Thomas Jefferson Kitts in *Advice on Painting from John Singer Sargent*, PDF booklet).

Chopra, Deepak, *Synchro Destiny*, 2005, Rider, 2003, Harmony Books.

Chopra, Deepak, *The Book of Secrets,* 2004, Rider, 2004, Harmony Books.

Cohen, Leonard, song: *Anthem*, album: *The Future,* 1992, Colombia Records.

Covey, Stephen R, *7 Habits of Highly Effective People*, 2013, 25th Anniversary Edition, Simon and Schuster UK Ltd, (first published 1989).

Csikszentmihalyi, Mihali, *Flow: The Psychology of Optimal Experience*, 2008, Harper Perennial Modern Classics.

Dyer, Wayne *Ambition to Meaning: Finding Your Life's Purpose: The Shift*, IMDb 2009.

Gilbert, Elizabeth, *Big Magic*, 2016, Bloomsbury Paperbacks.

Grylls, Bear, *Survival Guide for Life: How to Achieve Your Goals, Thrive in Adversity, and Grow in Character*, 2016, Corgi.

Hemingway, Ernest and Phillips, Larry W, *Ernest Hemingway on Writing*,1999, Simon and Schuster.

Henri, Robert, *The Art Spirit*, 2007 Basic Books edition, 1923, JB Lippincott.

Jeffers, Susan, *Feel the Fear and Do It Anyway*, 1997, Ebury Publishing, 1987, Century.

Jobs, Steve, 1981, quoted 201, *New York Times*.

Jobs, Steve, Commencement speech, 12 June 2005, Stanford University.

Kandinsky, Wassily, *Concerning the Spiritual in Art*, 1910, Dover Fine Art.

Kawashima, Dale, *Special Interview: Bryan Adams Talks About His Hit Career, His Songwriting, And Other Projects*, 2005, Songwriter Universe.

Matisse, Henry, *Jazz*, 2017, W. W. Norton & Company,1947, Teriade.

Mayner, Jonny, Honeycomb Law CIC, (creative law for creative people)

Milne, A.A., *Winnie-the-Pooh*, 1926, Methuen & Co. Ltd.

National Science Foundation, 2005, Study.

Neenan, Michael and Dryden, Wendy *Life Coaching: A cognitive behavioural approach*, 2014 Routledge, Taylor and Francis Group.

Occelli, Cynthia, *Resurrecting Venus, Embracing Your Feminine Power*, 2012, Agape Media International, LLC.

O'Donohue, John, *Anam Cara: Spiritual Wisdom from the Celtic World*, 1998, Transworld Publishers Ltd.

Oliver, Mary, *New and Selected Poems, Volume 1*, 1992, Beacon Press, 2004.

Pollock, Jackson, *Possibilities*, 1947, New York, N.Y. Wittenborn, Schultz.

Rideout, Annie, www.therobora.com, 2020.

Schmid, Richard, *ALLA PRIMA Everything I Know About Painting*, 1998, Stove Prairie Press LLC.

Schulz, Charles M, Peanuts comic strip, 2 October 1950 to13 February 2000.

Scott Fitzgerald, F, *Tender is the Night*, 1935, Penguin Classics, Scribner's Sons.

Smith, Zadie, 'Rules for Writers' feature, 22 Feb 2010, *The Guardian*.

Tolle, Erkhart, *The Power of Now*, 2011, Hodder & Stoughton 1999.

Wern, Lucy, *Hype Yourself, A No-Nonsense PR Toolkit for Small Businesses*, 2020, Practical Inspiration Publishing.

Williamson, Marianne, *A Return to Love: Reflections on the Principles of a Course in Miracles*, 1992, Harper Collins.

The Writers' and Artists' Yearbook, Bloomsbury Publishing PLC.